Disarming the Teenage Heart

helping teens navigate today's cultural minefields

Jeff Leeland

An Imprint of Cook Communications Ministries
Colorado Springs, Colorado

Life Journey™ is an imprint of
Cook Communications Ministries, Colorado Springs, CO 80918
Cook Communications, Paris, Ontario
Kingsway Communications, Eastbourne, England

DISARMING THE TEENAGE HEART

©2003 by JEFF LEELAND

First printing, 2003
Printed in the United States of America
1 2 3 4 5 6 7 Printing/Year 06 05 04 03

Editor: Marianne Hering
Designer: Ray Tollison

For privacy reasons, some of the names and anecdotal details in this manuscript have been
changed.

Library of Congress Cataloging-in-Publication Data

Leeland, Jeff.
  Disarming the teenage heart / by Jeff Leeland.
     p. cm.
  ISBN 0-7814-3870-5 (pbk.)
  1. Christian teenagers--Religious life. 2. Church work with
teenagers. I. Title.
  BV4447.L44 2003
  259'.23--dc21

                                        2003004657

Dedication

I dedicate this book to the women whose love disarms me most. First to my wife, Kristi, who disarmed my heart since the night our eyes met. To my daughters, Jaclyn and Amy, who mysteriously melt me as a daddy. And to Mom, who made my boyhood home something like heaven, I believe—a sanctuary of God's love.

And I also dedicate this book to Dameon, who perhaps is peering at all this through heaven's window. May the jewels in your crown be multiplied for Jesus' sake.

Acknowledgments

Publishing a book is certainly a team effort. I would like to recognize and thank the following people for helping to birth this work.

To Kristi and the kids, for graciously sacrificing a season of family time for my writing.

To Barbara and Mike Sharkey, for their ongoing love and support to the work of Sparrow Clubs, Dameon's legacy of love.

To the board, supporters, and families of Sparrow Clubs, who have made it possible for me to see the disarming realities of love in action.

To Lee Hough at Alive! Communications, who faithfully helped me to fashion the concept, and for finding a publishing home for my book.

To Janet Lee and Marianne Hering, who skillfully helped to sculpt the manuscript into its final form.

And to all those at Cook Communications Ministries who dedicate themselves behind the scenes to help change lives and influence culture for Christ through the written word.

DISARMING THE TEENAGE HEART

DISARMING THE TEENAGE HEART

CONTENTS

Introduction	Introduction: The Story of a Sparrow 5	
Chapter One	Surface Living, Deep Needs, and the Four Bs . . .15	
Chapter Two	Disarming the Heart: The Four Cs 29	
Chapter Three	Compassion: The Romance of Inner Beauty 40	
Chapter Four	Courage: The Heroism of Inner Brawn 55	
Chapter Five	Character: The Wealth of an Inner Bank Account . 77	
Chapter Six	Conscience: The Wisdom of an Inner Brain 94	
Chapter Seven	Teaching Kids to Do Heroic Things 111	
Chapter Eight	Four C Stories for the Literate Soul 126	
Chapter Nine	The Fifth C: Communities of Sanctuary 143	
Appendix One	Sparrow Clubs 154	
Appendix Two	Search Institute: The 40 Assets for Adolescents . 157	
Bibliography	158	

Introduction: The Story of a Sparrow

Introduction: The Story of a Sparrow

I have a constant reminder of the heroic capacities hidden in the hearts of teens. I see that reminder everyday. He lives and breathes and laughs and plays and "spreads his wings" like most eleven year olds. He's my young son, my sparrow—Michael, who is alive in a big way because of what my former junior high students did to save him. Believe me, beneath all the tragic news, shocking reports, and doom-speak we hear, real treasures are buried in young hearts.

Young people have been my business for a long time. My wife, Kristi, and I have five children of our own. As a public school teacher, coach, and administrator for fifteen years, and the executive director of a youth-based charity called the Sparrow Clubs for the last five, maybe kids have had to matter to me. You know—my job. But what an incredible difference they've made in my life. That difference is more than I could ever begin to repay.

On August 19,1991, my fourth child, Michael, was born. That same day I was offered a teacher/activities director position at Kamiakin Junior High. I accepted the job and moved my family across the state of Washington. But in February, six months after the move, an unexpected storm made our tight little family ship founder. Michael was diagnosed with a ticking time bomb inside his seven-month-old body—a rare form of leukemia. We learned that only a bone marrow transplant could save his life. But because I had changed insurance carriers with my new job, Michael fell under a twelve-month waiting period for transplant benefits. Even though his six-year-old sister, Amy, was a rare, perfect match, Michael was disqualified from the $200,000 coverage that could spare his tiny life.

My bumped-up teaching income was already spread thin supporting my family of six. Needless to say, if Michael's transplant couldn't wait until October, I had no hope of paying the required $175,000 cash deposit to have him admitted without insurance. Our baby had fallen through a very narrow yet deadly crack in the health-care system. So we began our journey through a jungle of red tape. We appealed to the insurance company, to the state ... and in quiet brokenness, to God.

As the new PE teacher I was "stuck" instructing the adaptive PE class, which had twelve disabled kids in all: three in wheelchairs, two with Down's syndrome, a couple with autism, and a handful with other severe physical and/or mental disabilities. Having plenty of practice at home playing games with my young children helped me invent simple, makeshift sports and games for these developmentally slow learners, a far cry from the advanced conditioning jock classes I normally taught.

Despite my heavy administrative load as activities and athletic director, I plunged into my duties with these kids. As I did, my heart slowly began absorbing a strangely sweet "emotional pickle juice" from the special-ed PE kids. Their innocent brokenness, heartfelt effort, and unrestrained joy for life created a culture that slowly permeated and softened my spirit. These kids with hard-to-imagine hardships had a real power to move my heart.

Michael was hospitalized several times with infections and fevers that spring of 1992. I well remember the anxious nights I spent by Michael's bedside at Seattle's Children's Hospital. Early each morning I'd head back to school—grudgingly—with Kristi replacing me for the day shift at the hospital.

Driving to work, my internal dialogue would go something like this: *Why am I doing this? ... I've had it with this job. I'm turning in my keys today! Stupid school—what good am I there? I'm financially ruined anyway. What's the use?*

Still sulking in a self-pity party, I'd arrive at school and survive until fifth period. The Down's syndrome kids, Ben and Heather, would typically be the first to greet me with hugs at the classroom door. And slowly my dismal perspective would begin to brighten in the warmth of these kids' spirits. As I began to see my own circumstances through the clarifying contrast they offered me, my ingratitude slowly dissipated. *I have a lot to be thankful for ... it could be a lot worse.*

I can still see Danny, his smile beaming from ear-to-ear, quite content and pleased to simply stretch his gnarled-up limbs on the gym mat and watch the others run and play. I see fun-loving Michael as he intensely competed with the muscular dystrophy that barely permitted his fingers to manipulate the motorized controls of his wheelchair—the clock winding down in his own battle for life.

No, I wasn't the teacher in this class; in reality I had the most to learn—this shallow student of life who called himself a teacher. How often I forget the things that matter most. Adaptive PE was more than my classroom—it was an uncomplicated and safe place, a refuge of rest from the burden of resentments I carried, a place to quietly reflect on my blessings. The power of the powerless is to disarm our hearts of anger; to drain the pain in our soul through the productive outlet called compassion.

Second semester, a seventh-grader named Dameon was transferred into my class. The school counselor placed him there because she recognized adaptive PE would be a safer place for him than regular PE. I would protect Dameon. Students respected me at school. I was the athletic director and a coach. Plus I'd played college football for the University of Washington Huskies in my younger years. Additionally, special-ed PE had this mysterious fence of protection that guarded it from the typical junior high aggression, ridicule, and pecking order. The stronger junior high chickens often "peck" to death the weaker ones with putdowns.

Dameon wasn't really disabled like the others—just a twelve-year-old kid who had trouble fitting in to regular PE, a place of high visibility, social vulnerability, and performance risk. He was physically overweight and emotionally undernourished at school, one of those walking-wounded kids who sometimes carried a chip on his shoulder. He scored low on the cultural curriculum of the hallways—brawn, beauty, brains, and bank accounts. He was definitely not one of those kids you'd see receiving an award at the end-of-the-year assembly. Very likely dyslexic, Dameon could barely read or write. He wore big, black stretch slacks with a big, white button-down shirt and a tie to school every day. He walked with a fused-ankle limp and sweated his way to school each morning. Dameon was a natural target for abuse once he got there.

First thing, Dameon took charge of pushing Danny in the wheelchair around the track when we did our warm-up lap for adaptive PE each day. He called it "boot camp" and quickly became a servant-leader in class. Dameon was my right-hand man. He was a battle history buff and would quote Winston Churchill often, probably from spending hours watching his favorite war documentaries on TV. I found this boy to be incredibly articulate, witty, and wise. His outlook on life and keen observations of people never failed to amuse and refresh us.

Dameon never personally mentioned his depression and elementary-school emotional traumas to me. He did talk about target practice with guns he'd like to own and his aspirations to become a bartender someday, which were inspired from watching years of *Cheers* reruns. But we had our own cheer time at the end of class each day, and Dameon earned his share of high fives and "Hey Dameon! Go Dameon, attaway, attaway!" accolades. He even earned the leg-press championship by lifting the whole stack in the weight room. Gradually, I could sense someone else was absorbing the same sweet pickle juice from the class as I was.

On Tuesday, May 12, 1992—three months after Michael's diagnosis—we received a devastating report. Michael's leukemia was rapidly becoming aggressive. He likely had only weeks to live without the transplant, yet the insurance company and state were still refusing to pay. Life-threatening transplant delays seemed certain. Our appeals to social institutions hit deaf ears. So we were moved to intensify our appeal to our Highest Authority, hoping and praying for Michael to somehow be miraculously healed.

I didn't attend the after-school staff meeting that next day. There, Kamiakin principal, Steve Mezich, shared my family's predicament with the staff. They were all deeply affected. The next morning, Thursday, teachers had stuffed envelopes with money into my school mailbox. Our vice principal, a woman named Detra, even came by our home and handed my wife a note of encouragement—with a check for $500 tucked inside. She hugged Kristi as tears filled their eyes.

After school Friday, 3:20 P.M., the life-changing phone call came into my office at school. Unbeknownst to me, word about Michael was spreading through Kamiakin Junior High like a virus—and the kid who didn't fit was the first to take action. It was Dameon's mom calling me.

Yes, I had her son in my class.

Oh, he'd heard about my little boy at school today.

What? He demanded that she take him to his bank … Dameon wanted to take out all his savings and give it to me to help save my son's life.

Would I still be there in twenty minutes?

I was momentarily stunned … *Yes, I'd be there.*

Fifteen minutes later, in came Dameon to my office with his mom close behind. "Mr. Leeland," he boldly announced, "you're my partner. And if your baby's in trouble, I'm gonna help you out."

Reaching out his fist, Dameon placed twelve five-dollar bills into mine, emptying his meager savings account in hopes it could help save my son's life. Sixty dollars you wouldn't trade for a million. This boy who faced mountains of adversity, made molehills of mine—and he sold the farm to help me. Words were hard to come by. I felt awkward, stunned, and indebted. I just hugged Dameon and said, "You're the kind of guy I'd bring to the trenches with me." To a war buff these must have been words of unmistakable honor. Dameon walked out of my office like he was twelve feet tall, his proud mom close behind him.

I was powerfully moved by Dameon's gift and immediately took the money and the story to Steve, our principal. He was inspired to open a bank account for Michael. That afternoon The Michael Leeland Fund was seeded with Dameon's sixty dollars of hope.

Spontaneously and almost miraculously, Michael became a real-life challenge in the hands of hyperactive, high-spirited, limit-challenging junior high kids at Kamiakin. Students, en masse, grabbed the sixty-dollar baton from Dameon's hand and raced to Michael's rescue—idealistic, unselfish adolescents with a passion to save my dying baby's life. These kids immediately issued a petition to boycott the multi-million dollar insurance company. They made personal sacrifices and created strategies to raise funds—walk-a-thon, raffle, donation boxes in every classroom, letters, petition, media pitches, and piggy-bank donations. It was compassion unleashed. And we were swept away by the incredible spirit of grace flowing from the hearts of ... yes, junior high kids.

Amazing sacrifices were made—the ninth-grade class donated their dance money that traditionally funded their end-of-the-year graduation party; Mary cashed in $300 of savings bonds; Kristen stuffed $100 of savings in a classroom donation box; Jon, a student who was perpetually in trouble at school, proudly brought in $26 for Michael after knocking on neighborhood doors. The spirit of protection for a broken child seemed to consume kids' hearts. The $175,000 wall of impossibility could not withstand the conscience, character, courage, and compassion of these teens.

Day after day students counted money, contacted the media, mailed thank-you's, and deposited donations into Michael's account. The goodwill epidemic quickly spread into the Seattle media, then to other schools and communities across the state.

From a second-grade girl who brought in a bag of pennies from her broken piggy bank, to an unemployed man who was $30,000 in debt and sent ten dollars when he heard about Michael.

From a Monroe Penitentiary inmate who sent a prison check for $25, to the total stranger who walked into the bank and made the largest single gift of $10,000.

From the insurance company employees who personally gave when their company, under contract, could not, to the eighty-year-old man who still washed dishes for a living and sent in one dollar.

Yes, each gift made a difference and tipped the scale in Michael's favor.

June 10: Less than four weeks after Dameon's donation, the Michael Leeland Fund contained over $227,000. In the eye of a hurricane of grace, we watched in stillness from Michael's hospital bedside as the awesome power of love struck full fury against impossible odds and miraculously blew away our immense financial barrier. Michael's life mattered—a broken little boy. Unlikely heroes—junior high kids—made a difference because they believed they could make a difference and then they acted upon that belief.

Dameon was given "The Character Award" at the annual awards assembly at Kamiakin Junior High on June 17, 1992. As he came forward, the entire gym full of students and teachers erupted in a standing ovation for him. After school that day he casually sauntered up to me and reported, "Hey Mr. Leeland, you wouldn't believe all the girls who are talking to me now!"

Weeks later, seven-year-old Amy donated her bone marrow to save her brother's life. My little girl's love overcame her monstrous fear of the unknown. That was nearly nine years ago. As I write, Michael is a happy and healthy, big-sister-teasing, soccer-playing fourth-grader. He's more than a survivor, he's living proof that something good deep inside kids can be unleashed against the brutality and despair that threatens today's kids.

Kamiakin students who were ninth-graders during Michael's ordeal, graduated in 1996 from Juanita High School. Their class magnetically attracted an unprecedented $1.1 million in scholarship money! Dameon graduated with honors two years later in a remedial track. He was also awarded a $3,600 scholarship by PEMCO Insurance Company—sixty times sixty dollars! For the next two years Dameon daily rode the bus downtown to attend Seattle Central Community College. He perfected a wonderful gift for woodworking—a craft he developed in his high school woodshop class.

I wrote Michael's story in a book titled *One Small Sparrow.* It was first published in 1995 and helped to launch the Sparrow Clubs—a nonprofit, youth-based charity seeded from Michael's miracle fund. Why named Sparrow? The small creature outwardly illustrates how we as human beings often feel. Most of us feel like we fly unnoticed beneath the radar screen of worldly importance. We all struggle with feelings of powerlessness and insignificance—especially young people. But Jesus is quoted in the Bible saying that God does not let any of his creatures go unnoticed. As the Author of all life and compassion, He notices our plight and takes every pain personally—and extends himself through every outstretched hand to offer true healing and hope.

The Sparrow Club casts a vision of heroic proportions for young people. By staging projects for young people to reach out and help children like Michael who are in medical crisis, we seek to tap into the private wellspring of compassion in kids' hearts and direct that flow of goodness into their public lives. A Sparrow Project is a "service-learning with compassion" curriculum tool to help teachers define and develop the private drama of heroism that plays out within kids when they publicly do what's right and true and good.

Kids are idealistic—they sense what could be and should be. They have great passion and energy to face incredible odds. But unfortunately, their capacity to act is often blocked by adults who fail to release them in their cause. My hope and prayer is that this book will encourage and equip moms, dads, and mentors to unleash our kids to do heroic things. It will help us treasure and develop the God-given capacities of conscience, character, courage, and compassion in young hearts.

Though I didn't see Dameon often over the last few years, he and I would talk on the phone and e-mail regularly. Every Wednesday at 11:45 A.M., we'd talk about Michael and the family. He'd ask how I was doing, philosophize about life, and tell me about his next woodworking job. Dameon handcrafted items to raffle at our annual fund-raising event for the Sparrow Clubs. Dameon also had a gift for crafting words as well as wood, especially in articulating the emotional needs of kids. We planned for him to come to work for the Sparrow Clubs someday. I could picture him going into schools and working with kids. He had a soft spot for children in medical need and for kids who need to heal by taking their eyes off themselves to help others.

In late September of 2000, Dameon took his first-ever train ride to come spend the weekend with our family in Oregon. (We had moved to work with the Sparrow Clubs.) He brought his prized, ornate chess set along with him. We had a wonderful time visiting, touring the area, watching TV, and playing several chess matches. Dameon even taught an eager Michael, now his little buddy, how to play. He decided to leave the chess set with us (a strategic move so he could come back again in the spring!). Saturday afternoon I interviewed Dameon on video. I was compelled to capture his views about Sparrow on tape. He always had an amazing ability to get to the point of things—to say in two words something that would take me twenty. We discussed how to get Sparrow Clubs started in schools across America. I asked "Dameon, why do you think we need Sparrow Clubs in schools?" His immediate reply was deeply insightful and simple: "Kids need sanctuary, a safe place in school, a refuge—a place where they know there are kids who care about helping other kids. Kids just need a place to heal."

Dameon and I had plumbed the depths of school violence in several conversations. He described it as "pay-back time," surprising me with how close to the surface old hurt feelings could hide. For the first time I really understood the bitter impulses of kids like him who'd been rejected, ridiculed, and intimidated in school. I've learned through my Sparrow Clubs work, for every kid like Michael who falls through the cracks of the health-care system, many more kids are falling through relational cracks at home and at school.

In my twenty-plus years of working with kids and teens in public schools, I've also learned at least two other things. First, everything that matters most to kids is rooted in relationship. Nothing can replace the refreshment they find in good friends, classmates, teammates, teachers, families, parents, and God. Kids are honest about their need to drink deeply from the wellsprings of relationship. Every kid needs the protective sanctuary of love from those who surround him or her.

Second, every kid is naturally bent to be idealistic, passionate, and cause-oriented. At the heart of every child is an atrophying hero who dreams of a call to honorable action. Kids have lofty visions of doing heroic things with the heart-gifts they've been given. Every kid needs to be actively engaged in sanctuary building—doing things to surround others with love, protection, and provision.

A month after Dameon returned home from visiting us, he became very ill. In three days, a staph infection that began with a leg injury quickly spread through his body. Tuesday morning, October 31, 2000, Dameon's mom rushed him to the emergency room. The infection was spreading into his vital organs. He was taken into surgery late that night. Early the next morning Dameon's mom phoned me. In shock, she told me that Dameon had died in surgery. I was numb with disbelief. Our Dameon was lost. We lost our Dameon.

Next Saturday afternoon the small chapel was packed for the memorial service. Dameon's parents asked me to officiate, something I was uncomfortably honored to do. My great loss and feelings of inadequacy were overruled by a greater debt of love. The service was homespun and straightforward—just like Dameon would've wanted it. We played a CD of the Snoopy piano piece—a Dameon favorite. Friends and family shared their stories and cherished memories of him. I read a Bible passage that reflected Dameon's personal relationship with God that had recently blossomed. And finally, with his parents' permission, I showed the seven-minute video interview I had taped of Dameon only weeks before. The sunshine of laughter momentarily burst through clouds of tears that misted our eyes. It was a Dameon moment, pure and profound. In my heart, our adaptive PE cheer echoed loud and clear: "Hey Dameon! Go Dameon! Attaway! Attaway!"

The day after Dameon's service, a Sunday *Seattle Times* front-page article caught my eye. It was an AP syndicated story from the *New York Times*. It was titled "Obese people still targets of blatant bias, hostility. Stares, gibes, rejection all quite common." The article quoted a woman named

Deidra and asked the reader to walk in her shoes for a moment … "You know that you dress nicely, that you are well spoken, that you are clean and friendly and funny and smart. Yet when you go for a job interview, your potential employer's eyes tend to sweep your person and fill you with horror." The article went on. "'I'm an upbeat and confident person,' said Everett, 33, 5 foot 10, and about 440 pounds. 'But you get kicked enough and even the strongest people say: "You know, I just don't want to be kicked anymore. I'll be strong in my own little world."' "

Dameon, too, had eventually found sanctuary in his own little world. His parents helped him remodel their garage into a shop. There Dameon began his own small cabinet-making business where he labored in a lonely love for the last few years. The article continued by quoting studies about obesity and left me knowing I had no clue of the relational aches and pains that Dameon had endured. I could not help but connect his perseverance in suffering to the positive impact he made on many others.

"Kids need sanctuary"—Dameon's word-picture was captured on video. What he beautifully articulated wove together my past threads of experience as a parent, teacher, coach, and mentor of kids. His words sharpened and magnified my vision for the vital work of sanctuary-building that awaited me. Two months after Dameon departed to dwell in his eternal sanctuary, I departed from the security of my career to launch Sparrow Clubs in schools across America. Today Dameon's influence lives on in a rapidly growing number of schools where kids are helping kids in medical crisis. And with this work, the possibility of true heroism and love is being awakened in kids' hearts wherever Dameon's story is shared.

> *Thus says the LORD: "Let not the wise man glory in his wisdom, let not the mighty man glory in his might, let not the rich man glory in his riches; but let him who glories glory in this, that he understands and knows me, that I am the Lord who practice steadfast love, justice, and righteousness in the earth; for in these things I delight, says the LORD."*
> Jeremiah 9:23–23 (RSV)

Chapter One
Surface Living, Deep Needs, and the Four Bs

Lori was a blond-haired, brown-eyed, beautiful teenage girl. She attended church with her family, got straight As, and was so popular in school that she was a student body leader. Money was not an issue either. In high school she worked over thirty hours a week, drove her own car, and wore the newest fashion in clothes. Whenever she watched MTV or looked at a magazine, she was compelled to go running to "stay in shape." Outwardly, she seemed to have it all together, but Lori was dying inside. She was empty, alone, and felt unloved. She tried hard to fit into an outer image that made her feel acceptable.

When she was three years old, Lori's father divorced her mother and left the family. He had no part in his little girl's life and went on to build another life of his own. She rarely, if ever, saw or heard from him. A deep part of Lori's soul withered away, starving for a taste of her father's love. In the fifth grade she started making herself sick after meals. She was afraid of getting fat and ugly. Deep down, she held on to the hope that her daddy would accept her back into his life again. She thought there was something she could do to make herself more loveable. She felt out of control over the emptiness she felt inside. It drove her to be even more energetic on the surface of life. But by her senior year, her outward appearance had deteriorated to mirror her malnourished soul. It seemed there was nothing psychologists could do to cure Lori's bulimia.

If there is one thing I've learned about teens it's that we cannot judge their happiness by outward appearances. Kids are driven to do many things to cover up their inner emptiness. As parents, we are quick to observe our teen's behavior, but rarely care to understand the influences and feelings pressing upon them. Their culture is like pickle juice, saturating their minds and emotions with harmful notions and mistaken beliefs. And every combination of people—from families, to neighborhoods, to schools, to communities, to nations—each has a collective culture that influences beliefs, which in turn influences behaviors. Parents must oversee the culture of the home. Teachers must care for the culture of the classroom. And every individual affects the culture or general flavor of his or her surroundings—to strengthen or weaken it, to sweeten or sour it, for richer or poorer, for better or worse. Good cultures provide a sense of sanctuary and bring out the best in people. Good culture is like the environment of adaptive PE, which had a positive effect on Dameon and me.

The inner state of a person's being is a culture too. It's called the soul. Kids are immersed in an outer culture today that makes their souls seem bland and unnoticeably weak. Their attention and interest is systematically turned away from who they inwardly are, from the real capacities they have within to change their world. Every choice kids make is filtered through either a weak or strong and right or wrong inner state. When kids have no strength of conviction in their hearts tugging at them to do helpful things, impulses and peers can easily prod them into doing harmful things. They must be put in touch with their endowed powers to know, to do, to protect, and to provide what is good for themselves and others.

The symptoms and consequences of this surface-living culture we live in today are well described by professor of philosophy, J.P. Moreland, from Talbot Seminary. In his book, *Love Your God with All Your Mind*, he wrote:

> Recently, the guidance counselor at a local public high school near my home confessed to a parents' group that the teenagers that have attended the school during the last ten years are the most dysfunctional, illiterate group he has witnessed in close to forty years. Our society has replaced heroes with celebrities, the quest for well-informed character with the search for a flat stomach, substance and depth with image and personality. In the political process, the makeup man is more important than the speech writer, and we approach the voting booth, not on the basis of a well-developed philosophy of what the state should be, but with a heart full of images, emotions, and slogans all packed into thirty-second sound-bites. The mind-numbing, irrational

tripe that fills TV talk shows is digested by millions of bored, lonely Americans hungry for that sort of stuff. What is going on here? What has happened to us?

Deeper Needs: Teens Yearn for Real Things

Deeper Needs: Teens Yearn for Real Things

I believe Moreland's concerns may be closer to many teens' hearts than adults care to know. No matter how hardened and trampled our teens' surface-living culture is, no matter how much attention is deflected away from their true inner state, no matter how much "irrational tripe" and image-hype mass media produces—deep yearnings for real things are buried in our teens' hearts.

Passion and idealism are neon signs flashing in the faces of young souls that should give us adults a clue. I constantly see what teens and kids can do in real-life dramas that involve helping children in medical crisis. When the stage has been set for these real longings to be called out from behind the curtain of surface life, real good things consistently appear from the inside-out of teens. Like the time a middle school group raised $5,000, secured a bus, and took a field trip across Oregon to deliver a gift of compassion and support to an impoverished teen named Sam who could only thank them with sign language due to a severely malformed face. Adults were amazed, but this simple gesture, this one neon sign, could be combined with many similar stories of youth heroics in other communities and light up our awareness like a Las Vegas boulevard at night.

Unfortunately, real bad things are often more readily accessible to a teen's inner hunger for realness than are the real good things. And the bad things get most of the press. But still, like vague memories, these deep yearnings for substance in life remain in teens. Our kids deeply want to know they matter and that they can make a difference. Their culture needs heavy doses of real good things to do. And the wisest caretakers of youth culture today will not only give kids good things to do, they give them heroic things to do. Kids need the real experience of meeting the real needs of real people. This, I believe, is the language that will speak to their deep capacities and romance their hearts into sincere pursuit of God, their real selves, and rich relationships with others.

Soul Language

The Echo Boomer generation (kids of the Baby Boomers) is experiencing cultural illiteracy to matters of the soul. This language that speaks to their deepest longings for realness is foreign to teens today. And we Baby Boomers have lost the art of reaching and teaching our kids' hearts with that language. As adults, we can barely remember and understand it, let alone communicate it. Because of our own surface-level lifestyles and habits, we have unknowingly created many roadblocks to a most wonderful, humanizing journey for our young—the discovery of who they were really made to be. Kids like Lori are starving themselves outwardly only because they have been starved of something inwardly. Culturally, we have nourished their bodies and nurtured their brains, but their souls have been expelled from school. We have animalized our youth, pushing them down impulsive paths of behavior with electronic media prods. We fatten them with entertainment and other junk food for the soul and drive them down paths to the marketplace to feed our own self-interested profits.

Government programs that throw money at surface problems cannot reach the root of soul malnourishment in kids. It's like the boy named Dean I had in school, whose family apparently couldn't afford school lunches, but I hardly ever saw him without a liter of pop and a big bag of chips. Free lunch programs are not the only answer. Unless kids' souls are freed from impulsive behavior, their money is just blown in other places—like CDs, videos, and junk food at school.

You've likely seen the cartoon of the old man riding in a wagon being pulled by a hungry donkey. The driver holds a whip in one hand and a long stick with a carrot dangling in front of the donkey's nose in the other. In similar ways our adult, market-driven culture speeds along quite well behind spending-frenzied teens who pursue the material things but never get the real sustenance their souls crave. Mass marketing campaigns drive today's teen consumers to spend over $250 billion a year pursuing apparent pathways to happiness and success. The average earnings and/or allowance of twelve to nineteen year olds has inflated to fifty dollars per week to keep them jumping through hoops towards surface things. Good looks, great bodies, clothes, cars, athletic prowess, GPAs, SATs, college degrees, and hopes for high-paying jobs—these promise much hope and happiness, but do they really deliver the basic things that kids need to build a good life? Teen-targeted mass media tell them so. Music, movies, magazines, and marketing campaigns emit powerful messages into the pickle juice of youth culture. In a recent newspaper article, *MTV: The Unreal World?,* the reporter asked teens this question:

"If all you watched on television was MTV, what ideas do you think you'd have about life?"

Here are some responses.

Seventeen-year-old girl: "Wear revealing clothes and look like you have money."

Nineteen-year-old boy: "Life is just one big party."

Seventeen-year-old girl: "You've got to dress up and wear lots of makeup and act sexy."

Seventeen-year-old boy: "Not just look like you have it [money], but have it."

It seems evident that a surface-living attitude has saturated the minds, emotions, and habits of teens. Youth culture needs wise caretakers, good teachers to help our youth learn to read the deeper meanings of experience and help them to understand and appreciate the real rewards of a good life. We adults need to relearn this soul language. Only then can we wisely and patiently guide a teen through these early and middle chapters of a long life story that ends well. It is a language that helps us all to rise above thoughtless pursuit of sensual gratification, to discern and value goods that may be hidden beneath pain or beyond immediate pleasures. But this language must be articulated in both principle and practice. As parents, teachers, and mentors of kids, we cannot communicate a language of wisdom that is not expressed through our experiences. Adults cannot transmit profound heart messages with simple head knowledge. The teenage heart hungers for real messages. It must be our mission to reach them where they are and deliver the message with good practice fueled with passion.

THE FOUR Bs

The website www.harriszone.com is a popular online opinion poll and message board for teens. What I like about the site is that it's kids polling kids—a great education for us adults who want to know where young people really are and what moves them. The site is quite revealing. And the kinds of questions they ask intrigue me as much as the gut-level answers they give.

A kid with an online alias name of "Zimmy" posted a poll that especially interested me. His survey question was this:

If you could choose one of the following for yourself, which would it be?

Intelligence

Wealth

Athleticism

Good looks

The three R's of Reading, wRiting, and aRithmetic have been the traditional symbols of the academic curriculum in American schools for generations. I believe that Zimmy's list encompasses the four surface-level goals that we find most young people pursuing today. I call these external ideals the Four Bs. They are the cultural curriculum of the school hallways today.

Brains or intelligence to win them prestige.

Bank accounts or wealth to win them pleasures.

Brawn or anything that wins them power.

Beauty or any appearance that wins them popularity.

Zimmy's opinion poll defines the external courses or directions teens must follow in order to achieve the most desirable ends this world has to offer. These four surface-world ideals seem to attract the attention and interest of kids like magnets. They operate like North, South, East, and West and give kids direction and motivation. But what I believe Zimmy is really asking his peers is "If I can't focus in every direction at once, where should I zero in? Which one of these courses will lead me fastest to greatest happiness?"

Here are the poll results:

54 percent	Intelligence	(brains)
18 percent	Good looks	(beauty)
15 percent	Athleticism	(brawn)
10 percent	Wealth	(bank)

The poll also contains a message board for voting teens to post their comments about why they chose as they did. With Zimmy's question, dozens of opinions are linked in conversation-like messages, one to another. Kids had a lot to say about these Four Bs—how a person could and should choose all four or which ones should precede others.

The postings poured in for two days. Then things changed when this message was posted by a kid identified as "hornet":

10/19/00 10:34:10 P.M.: How about wisdom?

The last two messages were added in response to "hornet's" question, "How about wisdom?" The final response came from a teen whose tag was "vow":

10/20/00 3:10:13 A.M.: Hornet, yes, why everyone forgot about wisdom, the most important to make the world stay still in peace.

Hornet offered an alternative to the Four Bs—Wisdom.

Vow connected "wisdom" to "peace." Something she knew that her world needed more than anything. Peace. A sense of sanctuary. Something foreign to the surface-level choices they had been given.

Poll ends.

The banter stops.

The silence is noticeable.

The halt in conversation after vow's posting seems more telling to me than all their other opinions combined. Why were the teens left speechless? Was it because they had little awareness of this language? Did she simply end the discussion by shifting the conversation from a horizontal, surface level dimension to a vertical, inward-and-upward direction that her peers were unfamiliar with? I think both.

Teens today need relationship with God. They need to know the reality of God's image that has been blueprinted within their souls. When teens compete against one another for the world's scarcities to fill the emptiness they feel within, they also must wrestle with their own external Four B limitations and frustrations. The Four Bs aren't necessarily bad—they're just inadequate in meeting deep needs. Shallow sips of surface-living cannot quench the deep thirsts for relational sanctuary that Dameon described. Horizontal pursuits cannot advance them in vertical dimensions of soul depth and higher love.

Bank accounts cannot buy rich relationships.

Beauty cannot attract another soul's pure affection.

Brains and intelligence don't guarantee good intentions.

Brawn is powerless to conquer our fears of failure and rejection.

Jack was a junior high boy who discovered the inward-and-upward dimension of love life. This new path helped him overcome an overly competitive spirit. I first came to know Jack as the kid who threw a flowerpot at the secretary's head in the school office. He was the "kicked-out-king" of Kamiakin Junior High. School psychologists say he had an "anger management" problem. Jack was ultra-intense and hypersensitive. He hated losing, fought a lot, and swore unabashedly when he performed poorly.

One evening I held a Fellowship of Christian Athletes event at school and invited a former pro football player to come and speak. When Jack saw the flyer he rushed to my office asking if he could bring stuff to have autographed. I learned he was a huge pro football fan and had even bigger aspirations to play quarterback in college and then in the pros someday. I told him, sure, that would be fine to get autographs.

The guest speaker shared about football, but more importantly, he told about his deepest need and highest purpose of knowing and growing in God's love through Jesus Christ. I could tell that a seed was planted in Jack's heart as he intently absorbed the message. Jack was at his new hero's side all evening. From that point on he visited my office regularly, retelling his dreams often and asking advice about football. Jack came from a broken home. Dad was long gone, and mom tried to manage her work and family the best she could. Jack babysat his younger siblings in their apartment much of the time. And he really seemed to enjoy our chats about being a winner in school, football, and life.

At the end of that school year of 1992 Michael's life was in crisis. Jack became a leader in his cause. Instead of throwing flowerpots, he threw his intense, passionate heart into the noble work of saving Michael's life. Tearfully, I still remember the day he came to my office with a handful of cash and checks that he had collected in his neighborhood. He would tell his friends, "Go door-to-door, raise money, and get everything you need, just make sure that he is saved!"

Three years later, Jack was in the audience along with other former ninth-graders at Kamiakin who were now moving into adulthood as I delivered the baccalaureate speech to his graduating class. Three-year-old Michael came up to the platform at the end to say, "Thank you," too. Jack stayed in touch with me for several years. I believe his hostilities were essentially disarmed at a heart-level by entering into a love relationship with Jesus Christ. Jack became a more peaceful, big-hearted kid who worked his way through school at a grocery store. He taught me much about teenage boys. I learned they really do need heroes to look up to—and heroic causes to bring out the best in them. They need good, tough and tender role models to help them become brave lovers of others and discover their true value in God's eyes. Most importantly, I believe they need a personal relationship with God, the greatest lover of their soul.

F rustrated and angry kids like Jack would do well to pursue significance in life ahead of success—to move from a place outside of self-focused achievement and into the realm of empathy in serving others.

Contrary to popular belief, God wired people to receive our sense of inner-worth by getting outside of ourselves, not from fickle self-absorption. I believe that the trendy strategy of boosting self-worth in kids by teaching them self-esteem mantras and affirmations is vain. We discover the treasure of our souls' worth when God's good and powerful nature is reflected within us. Our souls are reflecting mirrors and are made to reveal a more magnificent beauty, strength, richness, and position than the surface world can adorn us with. The most wonderful journey in life is to get outside our surface level self-focus and to begin a journey of discovering what God is like. And ironically, it is a journey where we discover our most lovable true selves, the real persons that God made us to live out and to love from. It's an eternal dimension and incomparable worth inside us. The seemingly absurd first step of discovering this sense of self-worth is humble self-abasement before God in service and cooperation with others.

Competitive Success Arenas

The root of Jack's anger problem, I believe, was that he desperately wanted and needed to feel worthwhile, to matter and to make a difference, to love and be loved. What fueled his anger was that his world could only know him by throwing him into competitive surface level arenas that constantly disappointed him. These surface level arenas are places of success, where we all know what it's like to be measured up against others in the world's eyes in order to be considered worthwhile. These competitive arenas include:

Education—Where we must compete with our brains
Economy—Where we compete with our bank accounts
Politics—Where we compete with our brawn or power
Media—Where we compete with our beauty (image)

Certain realities haunt young people like Jack in their competitive race for scarce rewards in the four arenas of brains, bank accounts, brawn, and beauty. The first reality is that the starting lines in surface arenas are not equally placed. Kids are born into this world with definite advantages or disadvantages in the Four B races for power, popularity, position, and possessions. From their genetic predisposition, to their environment, to their familial and national affiliations, they learn at an early age that competitive edges in the world have not been equally allotted. Life in the Four B arenas is definitely not fair. Research has shown that a high percentage of teens base their sense of self-worth on Four B gifts that are outside of their control. The Four Bs can certainly accelerate progress in our kid's public lives, but they cannot give depth, direction, or lasting fulfillment in their private lives. The Four Bs help teens reach externally defined goals, but may offer nothing to their souls once they get there. The Four Bs may give them power over others, but not a guidance system for aiming that power for their greater good. And, as a wise football coach once told me, "I'd rather have a slow player running in the right direction than a fast player heading the wrong way."

When our focus is turned to surface-living without connecting to God as our deepest Source, we are like dying batteries. Separation from God causes an inner state of emptiness and desperation. Our outward pace becomes frenzied in hopes that we can find something on the surface that will take his place and give us power. But life apart from God sucks like an eternal, big vacuum hose, consuming our hearts into tangible, yet substance-lacking vanity.

The deepest needs of our souls are truly like taproots, connecting us to our Providential Creator, to his creation, and to our creative capacities. But apart from our deep eternal Wellspring, our soul roots spread in all directions on the surface of life, enmeshed in comparison and competition with other people, sucking sustenance from the scarcities around us. Our deepest thirst is only quenched by personal trust in Jesus Christ. True faith, apart from anything this world offers, personally connects our taproot need to a deeply transcendent Way, Truth, and Life that overflows with his love through us and overcomes the hostilities within us.

The surface, competitive world of the Four Bs is a shadowy and shallow, unfair and unforgiving substitute for the Source of loving relationship that teens like Jack need—especially when their souls are wired to be aware of something eternally better. In surface living, young people are without fixed reference points that reveal a dimension to life that is most nourishing and satisfying to their human souls. God has blazed his nature trail in every teen's heart. We must know him whose image we bear in order to get our true bearings of purpose in life. The absolutes of truth, goodness, justice, and mercy are fixed reference points that help teens realize their true nature and navigate wisely through life God's way. These four soul-compass bearings are simply expressions of his nature and redirect our life's journey to fulfill our deepest needs and find our highest purposes. Without the unchanging guideposts of God's image we are forced to find our place and position in the world by comparing to and competing with other people. Comparison with others only leads us to the ultimate conclusion that life is unfair. Out-of-context competition with others to win the world's spoils leads us to ends that will only disconnect us from the love relationships we deeply need. In the surface world, we end up becoming victims or victimizers apart from having a vertical love dimension to our lives. Sour resentment and shallow skepticism come from living the horizontal life. But a simple shift of life focus to the vertical life adds a sweetness of satisfaction and depth of gratitude to all we do.

Secular humanism as the religion of non-religion continues to drive our culture to become exclusively horizontal and stuck at the surface level. It has permeated our public educational system over the past generation. It buries our deepest human needs beneath empty philosophies and theories such as evolution. It hides the human soul behind the external bushes of materialism. It offers atheists numbing relief from the painful notion of being accountable to and separated from God. It temporarily blocks their soul's painful sense of spiritual need. It excuses humans to blame that deep pain on every external "cause" imaginable. But the cost has been far greater than these short-lived benefits. This religion of surface-living denies the most powerful capacities of our real humanness. Secular humanism has animalized, brutalized, and sold out the souls of our kids. They are forced to get through a survival-of–the fittest minefield in order to win a sense of self-worth. The tools God gave them for building sanctuary are being forged into weapons for warring against one another. Their hearts are armed to do battle for control over surface-level things that are significant in the world's eyes. But this materialistic emphasis blurs their vision of higher human purposes and blinds them to the path where their deepest needs are met. Their God-ordained capacities go unused, their inner growth is stunted, and their resources for building healthy relationships wither away.

Jack needed to learn that competition in Four B arenas can sharpen his skills but does not determine his worth as a person. Every person has an important place in God's economy. Seeking to compete in the arenas of business, education, athletics, or politics can promote healthy progress and prosperity to a certain degree. Productive brains, bank accounts, brawn, and beauty make wonderful contributions to society. Fair competition in these arenas is fun and fruitful in raising levels of practical skills. But when we compete for things that can only be won through cooperation, even when we win on the external scoreboard, we lose something more valuable in our hearts. Problems begin when surface-level Four B competition is detached from the vertical dimension of loving God and other people. When the Four Bs become standards of self-worth the stage is set for increasing violence in schools.

It's often kids like Dameon who are targeted and blasted by put-downs in school hallways influenced by the cultural curriculum of the Four Bs. The human soul was never intended to enter such competitive arenas. Schools need to be sanctuaries for the souls of kids, not battlefields. But our kids must struggle up a food chain of social approval to earn a sense of significance and worth. They are vulnerable to deep soul wounds. Private arsenals of pain that can't be disarmed by metal detectors build up in young hearts. Young hearts are armed with cynicism, bitterness, rage, and anger. Eventually, as Dameon said, hurting kids end up hurting kids. "Winners" seem to get all the worldly goods—popularity, position, pleasure, and pride. And "losers" find other ways to level the playing field—sometimes with deadly force.

In 1999 Kip Kinkle strode into the lunchroom of a Springfield, Oregon high school, and unloaded his weapons and rage on his classmates, killing two and wounding several more. Before coming to school, he had shot his parents. The next weekend my daughter Amy played in a soccer tournament held at the same Springfield High School. The annual event is traditionally called "The Shoot-Out." It was a sad and untimely irony, hinting at how increasingly blurred and brutal surface competition has become in the minds of some kids. It should be a vivid reminder to every adult that we paint the targets of healthy competition in the minds of our young.

Having coached and directed youth sports for many years, I can tell you that we parents are often the very worst models. The higher purpose of competition is cooperation, for building one another up rather than tearing each other down. Every young person must know the vital role he or she plays on a team. And good teams promote each individual's growth and benefit. Every kid finds his or her worth by becoming a person of goodwill, sound mind, healthy emotions, and loving relationships.

The Four Bs Reflect Something Deeper Inside Us

The Four Bs not only define the surface-level, competitive pursuits in our kids' lives, but I also believe they reflect deep capacities for cooperation with God and others that are embedded in their souls. Their brains, bank accounts, brawn, and beauty are significant because they mirror more real capacities of God's nature within them. But the urgencies and distractions of surface life keep them from discovering the path and ways God deeply made them to be. And, more importantly, whose they were made to be.

Many young people like "vow" and "hornet" sense the shallow emptiness of merely pursuing intelligence, good looks, athleticism, and wealth as their goals in life. They realize their need for a new direction that only wisdom will guide them to. Wisdom points them outside themselves to find direction in mercy, justice, goodness, and truth. As teens pursue these realities they become more aware of God's good nature being reflected inside them. They begin to realize the higher purposes and deeper needs of their lives. Walking in the ways of mercy, justice, goodness, and truth reveals a pathway inside them for loving and being loved. This path leads to a point of decision, a crux of relationship with God in their hearts. It is where teens like Jack can discover the One True Source, Sustainer, and Goal of love and life who can be invited to abide inside them and with them forever, Jesus Christ.

Lori's Discovery

Lori volunteered to go on a mission trip the summer after she graduated from high school. Though she was withering away, both inwardly and outwardly, she traveled alone to Chile to serve in six churches of Santiago. Lori worked hard over the next several weeks. She cared for dirt-poor, bug-infested children and cleaned toilets. There was nothing outwardly loveable about these kids. They had no brawn, beauty, brains, or bank accounts. Nor was there anything self-affirming about her position. But Lori "accidentally" stumbled onto a path in her service trip that no psychological counseling session had directed her to before. Wisdom showed her the trailhead of a new journey in life. She left behind the deep pain of feeling unlovable as she empathically walked God's nature trail of mercy by loving outwardly unlovable ragamuffins. Lori became aware of God's compassion inside her. She abandoned her obsession for surface-level lovability because of something more beautiful she discovered inside her. By humbly walking God's love-path she unexpectedly discovered the Father relationship she longed for. She told me, "I have a Father in heaven who loves me regardless of how beautiful or smart I could be."

In the process of serving the downtrodden in Chile, Lori found new bearings. She lost her old way of trying to find love with a Four B map and compass. She stumbled onto God's nature trail of love. By the end of the summer, Lori also gained thirty pounds.

Chapter Two
Disarming the Heart: The Four Cs

Chapter Two
Disarming the Heart: The Four Cs

We must search for the kernel of virtue hidden in every flaw.—Goethe

"**S**ee what I can do!" The disheveled seventh-grade boy reached behind his back with one arm and twisted his other one limply around his back as he boasted, "I have cerebral palsy."

David had approached me with a group of four other teen boys who were mildly entertained by his public display. I showed interest in David's stunt, but focused more of my attention on the kid inside the disabled body instead. I learned David lived with his grandma in another town and had come along with her to help in the service event that day. It was a middle school project that Sparrow Club members were holding for their adopted sparrow named Krista—a four-year-old girl who was blind, developmentally delayed, and whose family was in financial crisis with her care. I thanked David for coming out to help us.

David tagged along with me and the other boys took off. As we walked, he volunteered information about the surgery he had recently to straighten out his left foot. I noticed he dragged it slightly. Then he told me about his friend and classmate named Steven who had cerebral palsy "real bad. He's in a wheelchair." David continued telling me about the anger he felt when guys at school called Steven a "retard." He wanted to protect Steven, to stop those guys, but he didn't believe in violence.

I liked David. He seemed to sense our relationship was a sanctuary for him; he felt safe enough to be open and honest. And from my observations, he had a heart to build sanctuary for Krista and her family as well.

Few people really knew David at the event. He could have easily kept his arm to himself that Saturday morning, tucked inside the tattered sleeve of his parka. But his stunt seemed ritualistic almost—a show-off behavior that shouted his desperation to belong. It seemed that this was David's way of numbing himself to the potential rejection of a newfound peer group.

Though my brush with David was brief, my heart poured out for him in a quiet way. As it did, I began to catch glimpses of inner gifts that were buried not far beneath his awkward behavior and appearance. In a sense, they reflected the Four Bs, but in a more beautiful, powerful, rich, and noble way.

In David, I saw glimmers of **inner beauty** that were delightfully manifested despite his external deficiencies. David displayed **compassion** and reflected God's mercy as he worked to meet the needs of a blind little girl. His intense desire to help his friend Steven, especially under the weight of his own apparent difficulties, attracted my soul's attention in a magnetic way. His compassion drew a sense of respectful affection from a deep place in my heart.

I saw **courage**—an **inner brawn** that impressed me by the way David used his power, rather than how much or little he possessed. It's a type of moral strength that reflects God's nature of justice, never taking advantage or exploiting the weak and innocent. Courage aimed David's power to protect and support a hurting child, one even more broken than himself. Courage makes kids tough in the face of their own adversity. The mountains of failure, rejection, and pain I imagined David had shouldered through his young life inspired me. In his own limited helpfulness, he refused to embrace a victim mentality.

I saw **character** in David—an **inner bank account** of values that reflects God's nature of goodness and made him a contributor at heart. David was there to serve by helping his grandma do the barbecue that day. The kind of clothes he could afford made no difference. His initial attention-getting behaviors were soon forgotten. He was the kind of kid who seemed to be making the best of what he already had. I felt enriched by David's honest effort and concern for the cause of Krista.

Last, but not least, I saw a **conscience** in David—an **inner brain** of higher intelligence that reflects God's nature of truth. David was likely no valedictorian, but he was sensitive to the needs of Krista, and he was shocked at how kids made fun of his friend Steven. He also had a conviction that violence was the wrong way to make things right. Conscience makes us sensitive to the needs and feelings of others. It's good at calculating the consequences of the choices we make. It writes an internal script of how duty and obligation should play out in our lives.

Like Lori, who got outside herself by entering into the needs of the kids in Chile, David had beautifully chosen to give of himself that day for the good of a blind child. I could see glimmers of light shining on God's nature trail of love inside him called the Four Cs. David couldn't articulate these virtues of compassion, courage, character, and conscience, but they were unveiled by his empathy for Krista.

By following the directions of mercy, justice, goodness, and truth, kids like David and Lori develop and use their inner Four Cs to walk the path of love. And love disarms the ridicule and rejection of peers and the feelings of revenge in young hearts. Disarming the pain of rejection, failure, impulsiveness, and foolishness in teens' hearts is more effective and much less costly than weapon detectors or any gun control legislation.

Empathy: The Doorway to the Four Cs

I have come to cherish working with broken sparrows—the Davids and Dameons and the kids in adaptive PE. They bring out something different in me, something deeper and better than when I'm trying to impress people who outwardly seem to have it all together, who have no need or use for me. Broken as these kids are, they help us to leave the ways of the Four Bs and walk in the ways to true love and fulfillment in life. For that reason, I believe we inwardly need other people's brokenness at least as much as they outwardly seem to need our help. In the presence of their brokenness, instead of striving harder in the Four B arenas, our souls enter into a doorway called empathy where we learn to use our Four Cs. Empathy is a doorway into sanctuary that Dameon's life exemplified so well. When Dameon entered into the brokenness of adaptive PE, and of my son, focus came off himself and off his inadequacies and insecurities. In this place of empathy Dameon's Four Cs were nurtured, invited out. They released him to become a heroic lover of others.

The story of a baby girl named Mandy illustrates how powerfully this doorway of empathy can lead people into a brokenness that brings out the best from them. Her innocent brokenness brought out more Four C service and goodness than could be achieved by our Four B status. The story is excerpted from an editorial written by Mandy's father, Marshall Shelley.

Mandy was born into our family two years ago, severely and profoundly retarded due to microcephaly. At first we desperately prayed that Mandy would develop some skills, but my wife, Susan, and I eventually had to accept the implications: Mandy would never talk, walk, sit up, or use her hands. She suffered seizures. She stopped swallowing, so we learned to administer medications and formula through a tube surgically implanted into her stomach. We never knew if she could see or hear.

Yet despite her handicaps, Mandy had an amazing ability to elicit love and point people's thoughts to God. People I didn't expect— teenage boys, a woman recently widowed, men and women who didn't usually exhibit much interest in babies—would take turns cuddling her. After a service, we had to hunt for her because she'd been passed from lap to lap.

In the neighborhood, the school, or the support group at Easter Seals, she steered conversations. You couldn't be in her presence without thoughts turning in a spiritual direction. *Why was such a child born? What is her future? Where does strength come from to care for her?*

In February 1992, Mandy suffered from a viral pneumonia her body didn't have the strength to shake. Despite our prayers and the physician's treatments, after five days I began to suspect we would never bring her home.

On Thursday afternoon, Susan and I sat in Mandy's room, taking turns holding her. A procession of people came by to visit. I sat amazed. My child was dying, but in her presence, we experienced revival, the confession of sins, and drew nearer to God. That night at 7 P.M., Mandy left her "earthly tent" for one "not built by human hands." In the weeks that followed, even as we grieved her absence, we continued to hear of her influence. One man I'd always considered uninterested in church wrote us:

"I never held Mandy, though I occasionally stroked her cheek while my wife held her. But I learned a lot from her. You've probably seen me standing by myself against the wall in the church lobby. I don't talk to many people. I feel like an empty well. I don't have much to say. But after seeing Mandy's effect on people, if God can use someone like her, maybe he can use an empty well like me."

Could a sightless, wordless, helpless infant ever be "successful in ministry?" If success is fulfilling God's purposes, I consider Mandy wildly successful. Mandy's earthly ministry lasted less than two years, but it touched eternity. And I suspect that's where real success is measured.

As tragic as Mandy's brokenness was, her small life became a doorway for people to get outside themselves. And by entering into her brokenness the best was brought out in her guests. A higher form of awareness was awakened, greater goods gained, inner strength developed, and beautiful feelings blossomed. The real needs of people around us release the good conscience, character, courage, and compassion from within us. Empathy is a safe place that invites our best work, where we express our highest art, and where we discover deeper rest for our souls. Empathy is an escape from the path of human competition and resentment that can happen any moment we are beat in a surface-level arena. It leads to a sanctuary where our own inherent self-worth is recognized and our heroic heart-gifts can be practiced and appreciated regardless of how imperfectly they are expressed or how we compare to others. When we exercise our Four Cs, we build communities of sanctuary and sweeten the pickle juice of culture. In such communities, instead of being armed with a competitive spirit of performance and appearance, we can be disarmed by cooperatively bringing out the best in one another.

In communities of sanctuary, our own brokenness is welcomed as well. Our vulnerabilities, disabilities, and inner flaws are safely ushered into the light of truth and love. It is where the harmful and handicapping effects of our self-protective ways can be clearly exposed and extinguished. Our emotional wheelchairs and crutches can be abandoned; the mistaken beliefs we cling to make our feelings of worth and happiness dependent on circumstances and other people.

In Four C communities, we walk freely in the strength of who we were made to be, toward the good we were meant to do. Instead of becoming victims or victimizers in this competitive Four B world of limited power, we become victorious and virtuous in pursuit of God's love. God's unlimited love flows best through unobstructed, empathic, humble hearts that express good conscience, character, courage, and compassion.

Four C Roots Precede Four B Fruits

Four C Roots Precede Four B Fruits

The Four Cs can grow most amazingly during the latent, adolescent years. Or tragically, they can wither away and nearly die. The Chinese bamboo tree story is a powerful metaphor to encourage kids to focus on nourishing and deepening their Four C roots before they can expect to harvest any good Four B fruits.

At first glance, the Chinese bamboo tree is an observably boring plant.

In its first five years the tree barely shows any visible sign of growth, becoming only thirty-some inches tall. Then in a period of only four to six weeks, the bamboo tree shoots up nearly ninety feet in a spectacular upsurge of observable growth!

Well-known speaker Zig Ziglar uses this natural phenomenon as a motivational lesson. Rather than focusing attention on the incredible outer growth, he asks his audience to consider what might be happening beneath the surface during those long, boring, and unspectacular first five years. The truth is hidden to the eye, but something very real is happening. During those early, latent years the bamboo tree is growing an enormous root system. It is invisibly building its growth spurt capacity below the surface, storing nutrients to support the visible surge it will soon experience.

Embracing the fact that **good roots precede good fruits** is a life-changing principle for kids. They learn that progress and success can happen in two different directions, in fruit ways—in the seeable, touchable, productivity-realms of life; and before that, in root ways—in the unseeable, untouchable, potential-realms of life. Like the bamboo tree, our spectacular successes most often stem from unspectacular habits. The Four B fruits can only grow and flourish from the Four C roots. As author Stephen Covey has written so well in his book, *The Seven Habits of Highly Effective People,* "Private victories precede public victories."

The roots of our souls need beneath-the-surface nourishment. We must fertilize our conscience, character, courage, and compassion with the nourishment of truth, goodness, justice, and mercy. The fruits of well-used brains, bank accounts, brawn, and beauty will eventually go bad or die without the sustenance and stability that comes from the soul.

Consider the painful story endings of many millionaires and celebrities. Many people who have wealth, sex appeal, power, and superior intelligence often are left holding thorns of deep disappointment and unhappiness in life. In order to maximize the benefits of the Four Bs and to prevent them from being harmfully used, they must be rooted in the Four Cs and nourished well.

Intelligence must be rooted in good conscience and nourished by the principles of absolute truth.

Material wealth must be rooted in moral character and nourished by the principles of real goodness.

Power must be rooted in good courage and nourished by the principles of justice.

Appearance must be rooted in compassion and nourished by the principles of mercy.

Over the past fifty years American culture has neglected its public root system. We have abandoned the Judeo-Christian grounds for our government and failed to infuse the values of our heritage into the souls of our youth. Everything worthwhile has been reduced to "outcome-based" production. Everything must be immediately fruit bearing or it is quickly chopped down as worthless. We're led to believe that only measurable things are valid, real, true, and worth considering. Yet there are uncountable attitudes, ideas, and feelings that we act upon every day that eventually bear fruit in consequences, good or bad. And if we honestly admit that these notions might be faith-based, ordained by our Creator God, they are immediately chopped down at the surface of public expression by a wrongly used sword labeled "separation of church and state."

The Chinese bamboo tree exemplifies that brawn, beauty, brains, and bank accounts are **fruits** and courage, compassion, conscience, and character are **roots.** The story has helped me to patiently encourage and nourish the heart capacities of many kids. It's fun to see them get excited about patience! The moral of the story quickens their hearts to know that latent, unspectacular adolescence offers root-growing power that can never be replaced. For kids like David and Dameon, their eyes light up with the hope that no matter how they outwardly measure up at the moment, that they have great potential for doing amazing things someday. From quietly invisible and unspectacular faithfulness in pursuing truth, goodness, justice, and mercy every day, great things will happen. The story gives kids strength and patience to press on in their daily quest to become the best they can be—not compared to their peers, but compared to their own highest calling and vision.

I appreciate the feedback I receive from young people who have read *One Small Sparrow* and also from those who hear me tell Dameon's story from my Four C lessons in schools. Recently, I received these words scribbled in a barely readable note from a seventh-grade boy:

> *It inspired me a lot and I look at people differently at how they make a difference in the world today and make Good because I thought I [was] worthless. But the speech you gave it's made me feel like I still have a chance in the world.*
>
> *P.S. I'm in Life skill to help disabal [disabled] kids*

Another middle school student wrote:

The story about your son and Dameon was very heart feeling. I was amazed on how a person like Dameon contributed his life savings to help your son as much as possible.

I never knew about the Four Cs until you told about them.

Everybody has some compassion, conscience, character, and courage even if it doesn't show.

Disarming Our Teens' Hearts

Disarming Our Teens' Hearts

Search Institute of Minneapolis, Minnesota (www.search-inst.org) offers cutting-edge research on teen experience, attitudes, and risk behaviors. In recent years, they have surveyed hundreds of thousands of twelve- to eighteen-year-old kids. We learn from Search Institute's research that

Only 20 percent of youth sense that adults value them,
Only 24 percent feel useful in their community,
Only 24 percent believe school is a caring and encouraging place,
Only 27 percent see their parents and other adults as responsible models.

Most teens today believe that we view them negatively. Many fall through the cracks of their communities and school hallways—low on the totem pole of relevance and usefulness. Many feel rejected, unsafe, emotionally disengaged, and abandoned; they feel they must find their way through life alone.

Our kids need us. They need to feel invited into the sanctuary of empathy and support that our Four Cs offer them. However, our own personal drive for the Four Bs—our passion for higher positions, power, pleasure, and pride—is perhaps what is wounding our kids most deeply. Our pursuits afford us the luxury of brushing more material breadcrumbs off our tables to our kids than ever before. Our kids are experiencing more widespread and profound internal poverty and pain than ever before. Suicide is the second leading cause of teen death in western society. Families are fragmented and scatter their attention in every direction of activity yet fail to care for one another's deeper relational needs. Misguided Four B values set the stage for the mistrust of our kids. Mistrust leads to disconnectedness and loneliness, and loneliness is the feeling of being unloved. It is the deepest kind of pain and poverty of the soul. Kids are hurting inside—and hurting kids hurt kids. More metal detectors at school doorways will not detect and disarm these arsenals that hide deep in kids' wounded hearts. Bitterness and anger quickly build up in kids who have no safe places to take their pain, heal their wounds, and find refuge in their vulnerability.

After years of teaching physical education and coaching, I still have much to learn about the soul needs of teens. But I did absorb a lot from those jobs. I know this—from dressing down in the locker room to performing up to the approval of their peers, gym class can be the most unsafe, threatening, and emotionally brutal place for kids in school. Dameon was certainly one of the most vulnerable ones. That's why he was put into adaptive PE. It was a safer place for him to be relationally. I believe PE teachers can be the most productive or destructive instructors of kids' souls in school because of the high competitive risks and emotional stakes involved.

I have learned that good coaches manage the relational dynamics of a team or gym class at least as well as the physical environment is kept safe. This doesn't mean teachers can remove every risk of ridicule and rejection in any class. It does mean, however, that they should have their mental radar screen tuned in to the relational realm of class. It means they should diligently respond to hurtful words and actions. It means they should use reasonable foresight to intercept potential incidents of harm. It means that the Four Bs must be put in context with the Four Cs for all kids. Competitive advantage, performance, and appearance need to be framed inside the bigger picture of a healthy community or classroom climate that is nourishing to every soul. And certainly, before this healthy place can be established and conveyed outwardly by teachers, it first must be ingrained within their own hearts. The doorway of empathy we choose to enter and the roots we choose to grow disarm our teens more effectively than the most sophisticated technologies. Disarming a hostile environment with our love, I believe, has less to do with what we do than with the kinds of people we become.

I heard an inspirational basketball coach once say, "The motivation of a team is measured by the morale of the last kid on the bench." How valuable do the last-picked kids feel? How important are the low performers on our Little League teams? How are the kids who wear Brand X shoes instead of Nikes treated, the ones who may be a bit chubby or awkward, but long to be winners too? How does the sense of responsibility to community affect our actions? Who are our downtrodden neighbors who need to know they matter too?

I struggle against the powerful Four B inertia in my own soul of trying to look good, be recognized, get the things I want now, and use my abilities to advance my personal ambitions. In my daily wrestling match with the world, I get too busy expending effort on my own aspirations to notice the needs of people around me. But I know God as my Coach. And as long as they are human, other people are part of my team too, no matter how disadvantaged or different they may be. The high morale and hard effort of less-talented benchwarmers in life are often a winning team's greatest asset. Good strugglers help keep everybody humble and grateful for what they've got. They point us to the real win that occurs within. You see, Four B self-interests can get the upper hand on all of us. Even though we may look like winners in the world's eyes, the Four Bs pin our hearts to pursuits that deeply defeat our life purpose. But God often uses the last-picked, under-dog players in the world to show us that victories in the heart are what make heroes. Winners are overcomers in the inner arenas of the Four Cs, not just achievers in the outer arenas of the Four Bs. Selfish success is an agonizing, lonely defeat compared to the ecstasy and thrill of loving sacrifice for the team. Lasting victory is a real lifestyle of love, not a successful event.

My lifestyle and intensity of pushing athletic kids to get the outer wins changed, I believe, when I began teaching adaptive PE. My daily routine still included competitive games. We exercised by beginning class with a warm-up lap around the track. And even though this did provide the disabled kids with some fresh air and physical exercise, in retrospect I think I became as aware of caring for their souls as their broken bodies. In one five-minute lap Dameon could excitedly tell me five stories as he pushed Danny in his wheelchair. The two Down's kids, Ben and Heather, loved to be recognized for crossing the finish line after their telltale pace of sprinting twenty yards in front of everyone, then collapsing until we caught up, then getting up again to sprint ahead. Maybe it took an edge off me when I recognized even the most athletic young men, like Jack, needed the same kind of care of their soul. They needed the very same affirmation for inner victories. The PE office became a place where kids could come and talk and be around coaches who seemed more human and real off the field. Kids flock to places where they feel safe and where they know they matter. Yes, even a PE office can be a sanctuary.

The Bible says, "Deep calls to deep …" in Psalm 42:7 (RSV). Teens deeply call for the Four Cs of our adult hearts, but we have only answered them with our wallets and well wishes as we brush them aside. Therefore their souls are left bankrupt by our lack of soul depth. I speak this, not as an expert, but rather as a dad who is desperate to do better. I have learned some very hard lessons. All the treasures, pleasures, and distractions we could offer them could never replace genuine emotions that prove we are attuned to them—our tears of empathy and our cheers of support. Heartfelt tears and cheers create a pickle juice chemistry that nourishes healthy relationships and becomes a sanctuary for our teens. I believe we must seek change in the chemistry of our adult hearts at least as much as we seek formulas to change our teens' behaviors. We must make our hearts a safe place for them. Only then will we have any hope of detecting deep needs and disarming harmful things in their hearts. The emotional investment for building Four C sanctuaries of our lives is high. But the return on investment—victimless schools and homes—is well worth our time.

Chapter Three
Compassion: The Romance of
Inner Beauty

No beast so fierce but knows some touch of pity.—Shakespeare

Shakespeare had a pretty good handle on human nature. We hear much about rapid changes in culture and technology. But it's rare that we hear about the timeless things, the beautiful things reflected in teen hearts that simply do not change. I have seen the truth in Shakespeare's famous quote in action many times—"No beast so fierce but knows some touch of pity." I've seen the fierceness in kids melt away in tears of pity; brutish young bullies ennobled by heroic giving. No matter how much violence we hear about in schools, no matter how angry or resentful teens might feel, no matter how great the pain in kids' hearts—there is a tender underbelly to every porcupine bully. One small brush with mercy can still bring them to their knees. Healthy impulses of compassion are still disarming to the teenage heart.

Compassion is the pathway or capacity in kids' hearts to transmit the power of mercy. Mercy is an attribute of God's nature. Compassion is inviting to mercy—like a romance. Compassion expresses mercy as an outlet to drain pain. Compassion is a reflection of God's beautiful nature within. Compassion has the power to change youth culture, one kid at a time.

The Impulse of Mercy

Just when and where the touch of pity will meet a person is hard to predict. My heart has been disarmed by it in the most awkward times and places—like at the gas station a while ago. When I went in to pay the woman, the arm and hand that took my credit card was deformed, and her face was a bit disfigured too. She didn't look me in the eye much, except for a few short glances. Maybe she felt ashamed or disgraced. I don't know, but she seemed quite helpful and happy to serve me. Nothing against a gas station job, but knowing the pay she likely made, I quickly figured this woman could easily have hidden away from the public eye, opted for some state-sponsored income. Perhaps she could make more money standing on a street corner with a cardboard sign that reads Please Give Me Money. But no, she was there serving me well, simply selling gas. And without her even knowing it, she is still serving me well, even today. And I don't mean at the gas station—her simple presence and countenance *at work* in a gas station that day was *at work* in me. And whenever I reflect on this woman's gift—behavior that was becoming to the beauty of mercy—it keeps on giving to me over and over again.

You see, I drove into the gas station that day like a fierce beast filled with frustration—I was running behind, my agenda overflowing; I had been thwarted by dumb drivers and bad traffic. But by the time I drove away, my frustrations had dissipated like darkness into dawn. One woman's inspiration did something to my ambitions, frustrations, and self-absorption. Her simple presence and humble service seemed to disarm the things that had held me hostage that day. My competitive agenda was put aside. I was freed up to move ahead more cooperatively because I was in a different place altogether, released from some unhealthy attitudes that locked me into myself. I entered the doorway of empathy and I left the gas station peacefully, with an emotional tank full of gratitude.

I believe God wove good mystery into every human heart. Mercy can romance us with untold beauty, intriguing us to behold a soul behind the veil of each person's outward appearance. This beauty is a powerful mystery. I wondered, and still wonder: *What power was it that disarmed me that day? How does this woman get along happily with her disability? Why is she taking a low-paying service job when she has excuses, or easier state-funded options not to?*

As I rest awhile and reflect on the gas station attendant, something about her soul still delights me. Good, hard work is always a beautiful thing. But pondering this woman's noble choice to simply serve other people despite her apparent flaws, serves me even better. She seemed to preserve a sense of purity and innocence in her brokenness—a powerfully disarming thing. Remembering Dameon always does the same thing, as do my thoughts of other young strugglers I have known. Often it takes a broken one who struggles or suffers well to direct our attention to mercy and something more beautiful behind the veil of outward appearance.

The Beginning of a Journey
The Beginning of a Journey

This human capacity of the Four Cs called compassion is the first to be introduced. Why do I choose to talk about compassion first? Because it seems as though image, appearance, and just getting noticed (whether it's for doing bad or good) is what matters most in the Four B world today. Hey, popular books even get written from prison! But compassion invites and releases a power within that can disarm and crack through this media-hardened, competitive surface of shallow appearance anytime, anywhere. The power of mercy can break through the surface-hardened nature of teens' souls in surprising, beautiful ways. It's an impulse, a divine seed really, that tenderizes the most callous young hearts and opens up any tough-kid exterior to the sensitivities of love. I believe these merciful impulses are like seeds dispensed by our gracious Creator who yearns to see teens blossom with their own inner beauty and heroism, to become brave lovers who know they are divinely loved.

Compassion carves a path of desire in our hearts to serve others. Along this path teens become aware of a deep thirst in their souls that cannot be satisfied by the surface world. It is a thirst for loving relationships. Compassion pushes teens' soul-roots to grow deeper and become aware of the other relationship building capacities inside them—the three other Cs: the inner brawn of courage, the inner bank of character, and the inner brain of conscience. When teens act on the impulses of compassion, it leads them to become more courageous, conscientious, and more capable of being connected to others in loving ways.

Compassion is the trailhead of a path extending beyond the doorway of empathy. It leads into another dimension, a new cooperative direction in life. It leads them to do what God requires of all people: "to *act justly*, to *love mercy* and to *walk humbly* with their God" (Micah 6:8 NIV, emphasis added). Compassion turns a teen's attention from the hardened horizontal racetrack of worldly competition to a vertical dimension, into a pathway of helping, healing, and love. It is a dimension that values place and direction over speed. The path does not end with them being "into themselves." The purpose of this journey is to be rooted deeply in God's love at the bottom of their souls. Then outwardly, God's love will grow to bear abundant fruitful acts of goodness toward others. Every kid has a place inside him or her to nurture this sanctuary-like garden of loving relationships.

Compassion Romances the Teen Heart

Compassion Romances the Teen Heart

I'm often asked to tell the sparrow story (Dameon and Michael's story) in schools where Sparrow Clubs have been started. I was once invited to share our story with a high school leadership class. I explained how the gift of Dameon had been passed along to a local elementary school that had adopted their own sparrow, a little boy from the community who had had four heart surgeries. The boy's family—four children and a divorced mom—lived in an apartment and struggled to stay financially afloat. Their phone had recently been disconnected. Dad had abandoned the family years earlier.

Not that I'm becoming hardened to what happens in kids' hearts, but I wasn't surprised to hear what happened later that day. It was another story of mercy beckoning another teen from Dameon's example. A girl from the leadership class approached the school Sparrow Club president, reached into her purse and pulled out a fifty-dollar bill. With mercy flowing from her heart she explained, "I saved up this money from my work to buy a new dress. But I realized that this boy needed help more than I needed a new dress." Compassion romanced this teenage girl to love mercy more than something to adorn her outward appearance.

I've seen an entire gym full of 750 middle school students express an attraction to mercy when they stood at a Friday morning assembly to commit to hundreds of hours of community service for a classmate with cancer. I believe it was the same romance of mercy that enlightened me to see through the veil of a gas station attendant's broken appearance. Mercy helps us all to embrace more real and beautiful things about other people when the outer stuff doesn't matter much anymore. Mercy is simply stunning to the soul.

Without compassion and love for mercy, we cannot see the real beauty in others that evokes wholesome affection. When the veil of outward appearance is all that matters, human worth is reduced to Four B marketability. Oh, that the minds of teens would be enlightened with the truth that God's unconditional love is the source of their real loveliness. And with eyes of mercy, teens will also see one another in this heavenly light. Mercy allows them to apprehend the inner beauty of themselves and others.

Thomas Moore wrote this classic poem, *Beauty*, long ago. It reveals the depth of this real, mysterious beauty reflected in the human soul.

> Oh what a pure and sacred thing
> Is Beauty, curtained from the sight
> Of the gross world, illuminating
> One only mansion with her light!
> Unseen by man's disturbing eye,
> The flow'r that blooms beneath the sea,
> Too deep for sunbeams, doth not lie
> Hid in more chaste obscurity.
> A soul, too, more than half divine,
> Where, through some shades of earthly feeling,
> Religion's softened glories shine,
> Like light through summer foliage stealing,
> Shedding a glow of such mild hue,
> So warm, and yet so shadowy too,
> As makes the very darkness there
> More beautiful than light elsewhere.

Superficial image may drive competitive beauty pageants of our surface world. But inner beauty cannot be won by striving against other people—it is a heart-gift to be nurtured. Real beauty is drawn out in our compassion for others, not won out in competition. It cannot be seized from someone else or swapped for something better. It cannot be owned or possessed. When we try to use it as a manipulative tool to self-indulge, the light goes out and we lose it. It is deeply enjoyable and admirable and accessible to all people. Beauty is pleasurable, but cannot be reduced to pleasure because it can blossom in the midst of pain as well. Real beauty is mysterious, satisfying us purely for what it deeply is, not for what it does or gets for us.

The heart of giving in compassion exposes the shallow emptiness of the Four Bs. The surface world may tell teens, "Take and get all you can as fast as you can—that's what will make you happiest!" But when they experience this inner beauty being drawn out for the first time—perhaps for a child who is innocently broken—and they give of themselves, they end up feeling much fuller inwardly than they ever have before. This is an experience that resonates with the truth of who they were made to be and how they were meant to live life to its fullest. It's a beautiful mystery—to give of oneself in respect for others and yet to gain so much in return. In this pathway, teens can begin to value themselves differently. They will learn to release their own hurts in subtly healing and gently powerful ways.

The touch of pity is a weird thing, isn't it? We can be walking along, minding our own business without a care in the world when *wham*—we're struck by it—the sight of a simple struggler, like the disfigured gas station attendant, like Dameon—someone who clearly has it worse than we do. We recognize it as the plight of a person who suffers with an apparent disability, disfigurement, or impoverished condition, but definitely without wearing the outer cloak of self-pity. They're not showcasing or asking for anything. They seem to be getting along just fine; they're even happy. Just then we are moved to a place outside ourselves. A place where we can see something beautiful reflected in the person.

I appreciate companies like McDonalds® and Taco Bell® for hiring the noticeably less capable to work alongside the apparently more capable. And even though I may have to wait slightly longer for my burger or burrito to be served, somehow my spirit is better served and my meal nourishes me more by knowing their bottom line goes a bit deeper than the company till. I bristle when teens mock lowly jobs and struggling workers. Hard work always turns a profit. And the greater profit is not in the measurable realm.

Mercy is something that comes out in the giver, for sure. It is also a chemical bond, a transaction between two souls. It is something that requires a contribution of integrity from the recipient as well. It reminds me of the lunch I had with Heather, a frail teenage sparrow with cerebral palsy. I remember how it took her a half-hour to get two minutes worth of food into her mouth. But the splendor of her simple effort wrung my heart like a wet rag. Her jerky muscle movements, hard-to-understand words, and severely contorted legs created more pageantry than any opening ceremonies of Olympic Games had ever done for me. Her teacher explained how Heather volunteered to restock books in the school library on Saturdays. I could only imagine how much toil it took her to be helpful. And her smile was contagious. I wasn't surprised that the project to help raise money for Heather's new wheelchair quickly swept through the entire junior high. I wasn't surprised when the students surpassed their goal of $6,000 to help Heather get through high school. At the end of the year, the leadership class celebrated with an all-school assembly and hoisted her to the ceiling of the gym with pulleys and a climbing rope. I believe Heather was quite possibly the most effective teacher in school that year.

True charity is always a double-win for both giver and receiver. Some broken people would drag the name of charity through the mud because they are also passive-aggressive, self-indulgent people; they want others to give to them in stead working toward a higher goal. Behind the veil of that kind of "brokenness" there is no real beauty to silhouette. And there is no light of goodness to shine upon it. But an innocent sufferer who, without demand or manipulation, in the midst of their carrying their own burden seeks not to burden others—this is the person whose inner beauty is silhouetted against the veil of their outer brokenness.

A good transaction of compassion has power to romance, captivate, and disarm our hearts with a sense of inner beauty. We can be thankful for being able to help. All parties are truly helped in a healthy transaction. Something precious from that relationship lingers in our memory banks—something beautiful to reflect upon. God plants the seeds of pity in givers' hearts, but receivers have a responsibility too. They can help nurture the growth of compassion by their commitment to something higher than their immediate relief. By nurturing this impulse of pity, and not abusing it, this small seed can grow to become a fruitful learning experience, where there is bountiful goodness and beauty for everyone.

Compassion Drains the Pain in Teens' Hearts

Compassion disarms the harmful power of pain in the teenage heart. It relieves internal pain and releases deeper heart-gifts that build others up. Teens discover there's something inside them that's more lasting and genuine than the materialistic glitter sprinkled around them. And when they tap into the wellspring of loving relationships, the desire for self-indulgent junk begins to fall from their hearts like leaves in the dead of winter.

The best example I can think of is Steve Mezich, the principal at Kamiakin Junior High—the guy who hired me and "stuck me" with teaching adaptive PE. It was Steve who took it on himself to share my predicament at a staff meeting, who took Dameon's money to the bank and started an account. Steve gave the kids at Kamiakin something heroic to do, and grew to become my close buddy and Sparrow Clubs board president. Steve—who five years ago lost his team roping partner, his only son, Luke, in a tragic car accident.

Yes, Steve, my friend, a guy who's gone many extra miles for me, shared with me in his own cowboy style something extremely wise. He told me the three greatest things God had taught him through his pain:

Everybody is fragile, hurting, and broken somewhere deep inside.

Everybody needs something to feel important about, and to know that their life makes a difference to someone.

Everybody needs an outlet—some way to share their pain.

Yep, Steve is one tough dude who has been deeply tenderized—who is not ashamed of shedding tears or afraid being real—who drains the pain in his heart by serving others, by comforting parents of our fallen sparrows. He's a guy who, every Father's Day for the past five years, puts on the Luke Mezich Memorial Team Roping Event to benefit kids and families who are broken too. Steve is doing something powerful with his pain, making a big difference in the lives of so many kids. His tragedy has become a beautiful, unfolding story that is making a difference for good.

The Deepest Needs in the Human Soul

Lesson One: "Everybody is fragile, hurting, and broken some-where deep inside.

Steve's wise observation helped me to realize that every soul we meet is a candidate for compassion. And the truth is that we're all broken to some degree. I think we'd all do well in a place like "adaptive PE for the soul," where everyone has their place, where everyone simply does their best—and we all cheer one another's success.

In the biography, *Teresa of Calcutta,* by D. Jeanene Watson, Mother Teresa is quoted in a conversation with a visiting dignitary.

Mother Teresa said: "For all kinds of diseases there are medicines and cures. For loneliness, the best cure is love."

Lady Jordan then asked, "What is the worst disease? Leprosy?"

"The biggest disease today is not leprosy, but rather the feeling of being unwanted, uncared for, and deserted by everybody. Outcasts are found at every stage of life, from the aged to the newborn infant."… Teresa explained to the visitor from England, "This is the worst disease. People have no time for their children, no time for each other, no time to enjoy each other. Jesus himself experienced this loneliness. He came among his own and his own received him not. It hurt him then, and it has kept on hurting him."

We all share this relational brokenness or loneliness at some level. But there are differences in brokenness that are important for us to understand too. The child with cancer, the boy with a disability, the disfigured woman: each has something in common—their fragileness is visible. Like my son Michael. As a baby with leukemia, he was a compassion magnet. He was a cute, innocent, blond-haired baby. His life was at stake. He needed help fast—and there was something practical that people knew they could do to make a difference. Over the years, being in the Sparrow Clubs youth-charity "business," I can see these particular things in Michael's "profile" that seemed to yank the most beautiful acts of kindness right out of people.

But for every Michael, there are a thousand Dameons wandering the school hallways—as needful of compassion to save them emotionally as Michael was in physical need. Their emotional needs are acute, but they are "un-cute." They are hurting and lonely. They are non-athletic, poor, and struggle with learning in the formal school setting. These are the invisible walking wounded, the make-fun-of targets, the disenfranchised, the nobodies who go unnoticed, the perpetual benchwarmers of school life.

We adults can all go back there, if we dare to remember our own junior high days. We can go there now, just pondering our place of employment. The core issues are the same as our kids feel—a sense of being cheated, left out, and hurt because other people get more attention or better opportunities than we get. We unconsciously grade our coworkers' or competitors' advantages and our disadvantages in terms of the Four Bs. Believe it or not, the "Kings and Queens of the Four B Hill" are in the same emotional boat we are in, but with one major difference—many have already climbed those corporate ladders to success only to realize what they deeply wanted wasn't there after all. False hopes contribute to both our illusions and our disappointments! What we all deeply want and need is hidden in loving relationship with God and others.

Lesson Two: "Everybody needs something to feel important about, and to know their life makes a difference to someone."

The heartbeat of relationship is loving and being loved. Most deeply, we need to know that our lives matter and that we can make a difference in the lives of others. This is the antidote to the dreaded disease of the human soul that Mother Teresa diagnosed. It's the disease of disconnectedness. Just as our physical heart is a hollow muscle that facilitates the flow of lifeblood through us, in a soul-way, our relational heart is a conduit for the flow of love in and through us. Helping to meet the needs of one another by exercising our heart-gifts is the lifeblood of our souls and our relationships—we simply cannot live healthy lives without love. The heartbeat of our soul is to love and be loved.

I'm still a physical education and health teacher at heart. I think that's why many of my word pictures relate my understanding of the soul to my understanding of the body—like the Four Cs relate to the Four Bs. Now I'm not necessarily an expert in body and soul, just a former coach and current youth-charity director. Someone who has seen bodies and souls in action, someone who loves to learn and teach about rightly using, caring for, and being good stewards of all the amazing human capacities of both body and soul.

I not only have studied the human body and the principles of fitness, but also for many years I trained young athletes in the disciplines of advanced conditioning for peak athletic performance. What I know is that the most basic and important component of fitness is cardiovascular endurance—the fitness of the heart and lungs. While it is the most beneficial component overall, it is probably the least fun and most painful part of training. Students love to max out on the bench press in front of their friends, but they hate to run the mile. They enjoy scrimmage, but they despise wind sprints. But that's what coaches are for—right? I heard the great football coach, Tom Landry, once say something like this, "A good coach will make you do what you don't want to do, so that you can get what you really want to get." That's a good one for us parents to remember too.

Over time, after students learn to train their heart and lungs regularly at the right pace, to monitor their progress, and to celebrate the small victories of progress, they inwardly change. They become more resilient to the pain of training over all. They become better at performing. They practice harder, play with more energy, and recover faster. Cardiovascular disciplines built a base for higher-level training and achievement in all other areas.

In a similar way, I believe the heart of our soul benefits from disciplined training as well. Every kid has heart-gifts to give, and every community needs their contribution. And compassion is the best practice to exercise those gifts. When kids enter into the brokenness of others, it brings out the best in them. But perhaps the biggest difference we can make is to inspire others to use their gifts to the fullest. That's where kids like Dameon and David can have a most profound effect on their communities. When kids give out of their Four B skills and strengths, it produces measurable and admirable results. But when they give out of their brokenness, it releases a flood of inspiration that moves others to release their gifts as well, making an even greater measurable difference.

Lesson Three: "Everybody needs an outlet—some way to share their pain."

Most counseling experts would agree, even though they may not phrase it Steve's way. When we practice compassion, we seem to be put in touch with our own pain. I have seen this in school settings. Counseling offices can fill up with kids whose own deep woundedness surfaces when they've been touched with pity for another student or child. This is a good thing, however, in bringing issues to the surface to be dealt with in healthy ways. Like cardiovascular conditioning, kids learn to tolerate and overcome pain when they experience the good purposes that will follow.

Even seemingly petty teenage pain can be drained by compassion. Cindy was a fifteen-year-old freshman in high school. After the alarm clock awoke her for school one morning, the mirror alerted her to three big zits that had surfaced on her face overnight. The usual worries a school day brings can be devastating enough for a teenage girl. Before she left for school, Cindy demanded that her mother make an appointment with the skin doctor. The pressure to be pretty and popular weighs much heavier on teens' hearts than we parents care to know. Three pimples can quickly steal their self-confidence, and the threat of a chronic bad complexion is even worse.

After doing her best to cover up the life-threatening blemishes, Cindy went to school, painfully self-conscious of every casual glance that came her way. She braced herself for rejection that day. Every unheard word in the hallway was certainly aimed at her, she believed. She definitely knew what crowd of "friends" to avoid. But in third period class, a girl named Rebecca captured her eye. Rebecca was a quiet classmate who had been Cindy's friend in the fourth grade. Unfortunately she faced a more difficult battle with her complexion. Judging from Rebecca's inexpensive clothes, her parents definitely couldn't afford to see a dermatologist like Cindy could. Cindy recalled how the boys in middle school called Rebecca a dog and tagged her as a loser in the brief season she tried to fit in.

The crack in Cindy's outward appearance (a few pimples) was really a rich gift; it opened her emotional eyes to consider Rebecca's pain in third period class that day. Cindy noticed something more real and beautiful about her former elementary school friend. Rebecca seemed to be more at peace with her appearance than Cindy was with hers. She had come into unpopularity with certain cliques at school, yet she remained friendly. Rebecca still said hi in the hallways and was nice despite the fact Cindy and her popular group of friends "dissed" her. In contrast to Cindy's daily turmoil to outwardly measure up to peer approval, Rebecca's unpopularity now appeared to be a peaceful retreat away from the surface games others struggled with. Cindy's minor blemishes helped her to feel the pain of rejection Rebecca must have experienced. She felt sorry for how she had judged Rebecca and how she chose to distance herself. She felt ashamed of the way she joined in the ridicule of other kids for their outer flaws.

Cindy considered a small gesture of acceptance that she could extend to Rebecca. *Maybe I'll sit with her at lunch sometime soon,* Cindy thought. She was sensitized to Rebecca's pain because of her own pain that day. A bad thing became a good thing because it triggered a moment of unconditional love and acceptance between two very worthwhile girls who needed to be reaffirmed of their inner lovability.

When teens focus and compare their conditions to others who are above them on the Four B ladder of success, they feel compelled to open the anger pathway to vent their hurts. But when a teen considers the conditions of someone less fortunate, their hearts and minds can quickly become open conduits to release hidden hurts in the form of suffering love. Compassion fathoms the depths of pain in another's soul; it opens a floodgate and drains the pain and opens them to the soothing and healing fresh flow of love.

The Discipline of Compassion

I've seen what happens when a tough teen is surprised by mercy in his heart. But compassion can and should also become intentional, taken from the realm of impulse to become an inner discipline. Then it can be linked to other disciplines of the soul—courage, character, and conscience. It can be the impulse that introduces them to their Four Cs. Compassion, also known as pity, love, mercy, or kindness, is often associated with weakness, gushiness, or doormat-like defenselessness. On the contrary, true compassion is everything but the above. And these false ideas must be dispelled, especially in the mindset of boys. Compassion is a very powerful tool in the hearts of heroic youth who will fight to do what's right and good. Compassion has a "Jiu-jitsu" effect on evil.

Jiu-jitsu is the Japanese martial art of fighting without weapons. *Jiu* means "gentleness" or "giving away" and *jitsu* means "art" or "practice." It is the skillful, systematic technique of using the strength and weight of an opponent, turning and leveraging it to his own disadvantage. It overpowers an opponent by redirecting his force in the way you want it to go. It's real toughness with a tender exterior.

The hidden force behind anger or fierceness in teens is the same power that can be turned into "pity" for others. Fierceness and pity are fueled by the same deep pain in the heart. Compassion uses the pain we contain to fuel the higher purpose of helping others. In its Latin roots, compassion means to "suffer with" another. It is a divinely endowed pathway in the human heart where pain is turned into pity and drains with sorrow for another person's woe. It moves a person to act with kindness. We are often most able to comfort others who are experiencing the same kind of pain that we have experienced. Compassion can open up and tenderize any hardened and callous young heart. With its trained eye, compassion sees through appearances to behold inner beauty. With its trained ear, it is attuned to the heart-cry softly sounding in another person's soul.

Because of the unrealistic external standards of the Four Bs, all kids feel frustrated, defeated, or excluded to some degree. Some kids are hurting more than others—a condition that gives them a greater capacity to make a greater impact for evil or for good, either through meanness or kindness. Dameon was a beautiful example of a boy who was emotionally beat up because of his lack of outward beauty. But he chose the tougher pathway of tenderly giving despite the excuses he could have used to vent his pain the other way. Dameon made no excuses to return evil for evil, he simply exercised the capacity of his soul to do jiu-jitsu on evil and overcome it with good. I believe it is a capacity that every human is capable of and responsible to practice. Compassion is an art form of choice, not mere emotion. It is the human capacity to drain pain in a good way. It takes practice to develop this skill and strength of the soul. But it is something they can and must learn to do; otherwise they will default and succumb to the weaker, easier pathway of vengeance.

The pain in young hearts is at epidemic proportions today because of eroding morals and crumbling homes. As one youth counselor expressed, "Our culture is toxic to teens." Hurting kids hurt kids. But where are the "jiu-jitsu masters" who can help turn the pain into gain? Are there no skilled trainers who can teach kids the powerful art of practicing compassion? What are we willing to do to have more school triumphs like Kamiakin? And will those triumphs prevent future tragedies like the murders and suicides at Colorado's Columbine High School? Can the pain in youth culture be turned into a movement of compassion?

I've seen it done. Teens can learn to skillfully redirect the force and weight of pain that energizes evil and violence into acts of kindness. By training in the art of compassion, young people will recognize a paradoxical opportunity: the depth of their sacrifice in doing good magnifies the impact of their love.

Compassion Is the Reflection of Inner Beauty

On the banks of the beautiful Deschutes River in Central Oregon near where we live, there is a peaceful place of reflection called Mirror Pond. It is located at a lazy bend in the river where the waters run slow and deep. A long time ago a wooden platform was built right there at water's edge—a deck that faces west toward a jagged mountain called Brokentop.

From the platform, sunrise at Mirror Pond is an experience of incredible beauty. In morning stillness, the mountain is magnified across the quiet waters. Brokentop's broken image leaps out in a fiery glow and grips onlookers with the wonder of God's handiwork: still waters, clear skies, morning sun—and a perfect point of view. The platform is the handiwork of some wise observer who long ago recognized this perspective and built a platform in just the right place. The stage is set for Mirror Pond's natural gift of reflective beauty to be revealed, new every morning. Many people come there to find refreshment and rest as they ponder the image of a broken mountain on quiet waters.

Real beauty is in the face of God, reflected in his creation and especially the souls of his people, inviting us to be restored in him. From the very beginning it was so. He seems to exercise his creative powers in the simplest, silent, and subtle ways—rising tides, sprouting seeds, whispering new life into a mother's womb.

The soul of man is similar to the image in Mirror Pond, something that reflects the beauty of God's image on the horizon. And Creation is like a veil, something we can see through dimly to the silhouette of Someone on the other side. And like the reflection in Mirror Pond, God's awesome beauty is best reflected by the peaceful stillness inside us, not by our outward appearance. Every person is a mirror-pond, really; and compassion is a reflecting place where God's goodness and beauty are pictured.

The touch of pity is powerful in the teenage heart. Compassion moves teens to give of themselves with idealism and strength. It can blossom into a beautiful thing in our homes, schools, churches, and communities. Compassion is inner beauty that reflects the goodness of God. And compassion is a platform from which we can reflect on the awesome beauty of God and his love for each one of us. By reflecting on true beauty, we can become inspired to step outside ourselves and enter into the pain of another. And God's beauty is reflected in us.

The power of compassion disarms pain in the heart.

Chapter Four
Courage: The Heroism of Inner Brawn

Chapter Four
Courage: The Heroism of Inner Brawn

O! it is excellent
To have a giant's strength,
but it is tyrannous
To use it like a giant.
—Shakespeare

The high school classroom was filled with sophomores and juniors. I closed my storytelling time about the heroic things kids can do by passing around a picture of Dameon holding three-year-old Michael. Scanning the room, I noticed a large girl sitting in the back row wiping tears from her eyes. After class I mentioned the girl to her teacher, a caring woman named Mary, who was also the Sparrow Club advisor at school. I must have sensed that this girl identified with Dameon's pain and needed a safe place to drain it. Mary and I agreed that she might benefit from being included in the club. Maybe she could find her place in helping the school's adopted sparrow—a baby named Vern. The little guy had already had multiple surgeries and currently struggled to breathe. His family struggled to stay afloat financially since his mother needed to stay home to care for her broken baby.

Nearly two years passed before Mary contacted me and shared the heart-wrenching but heroic story of Lindsey Wilcox, the girl who cried in Mary's class. The day after I shared Dameon's story, Mary invited Lindsey to join Sparrow Club. Lindsey's heart was magnetized to the cause of helping the school's adopted child. Few at school saw Lindsey's tender heart in action or cared about her unwavering devotion and dedication to helping Vern. And, like many of her classmates, I knew nothing of Lindsey's real story until Mary called me.

News had spread through the area that a teenage girl had died in a house fire. The small trailer where she lived with her elderly father had erupted into flames. Thinking only to rescue him, the girl worked her way to the back bedroom. The father, however, had already found his way out. Tragically, she was trapped and did not make it back out.

A front-page newspaper article told the story of Lindsey Wilcox's brave deeds. In life she had given fully; in death she inspired others to donate to Sparrow Clubs in her memory.

Love and heroism go hand in hand. They dwell in the same realm of inwardness and upwardness. They have little to do with outwardness. I believe Lindsey tapped into that realm, the most powerful force in the universe—sacrificial love. God is love. This is the Source we are directed to in the Bible, as it is written: "May your roots go down deep into the soil of God's marvelous love. And may you have the power to understand, as all God's people should, how wide, how long, how high, and how deep his love really is" (Eph. 3:17–18 NLT).

Survival-of-the-fittest culture is non-sacrificial. In the world's way, brawn is power to exploit the less powerful for personal gain. In God's way, courage is our heroic power to sacrificially protect from harm what is good—especially where it concerns the weak and innocent. In this world, good things are attacked by evil. For some reason the world just isn't fair—life is tough. Courage is a teen's moral muscle fiber to resist evil, to be resilient, and resolve to overcome evil with good despite pain and discouragement.

Compassion blossoms in young souls. It is where the impulse of mercy takes root and bears the fruit of love for others. This fertilizes the development of the second heart-gift in every teen—the inner brawn of courage.

Courage is the capacity of young people to be Davids, not Goliaths, to bravely use their God-given strengths in skillful and strategic ways, to uphold justice, and to help the vulnerable and weak and oppressed rather than to take selfish advantage of them. Young people must be inwardly strong enough to be intentionally vulnerable. Courage stands against the tyrants who trample other people's God-given rights. Courage stands against the terrorism of brutality and the corruption of bribery. It disarms evil powers that make the world unsafe and unfair for the weak and oppressed. Courage disarms needless pain and fear that coerce people into returning evil for evil. It is heroism operating in young hearts that will prevent the tyranny of powerful giants from trampling kids in school hallways. Teens need to heed the call of courage and arm their souls with strength for noble action—to defend and protect liberty and justice for all.

Chivalry versus Brutality

Chivalry versus Brutality

Teens would do well to enroll in "Knight School" today. During medieval times, the knighthood was a powerful order of ordained men who protected the domains and interests of their kings, lords, and the church. They committed themselves to a code of ethics and behavior called chivalry. The code of chivalry defined the qualities of an ideal knight. These qualities included bravery, honor, courtesy, respect for women and children, protection of the weak, generosity, and even fairness towards their enemies. Many of these knights were also soldiers at heart, and they, too, were tempted to use their strengths to spoil, plunder, and victimize their opponents. The code of chivalry put the knights' resources under subjection to higher purposes than their shallow self-interests. But the code also did another profound thing. Chivalry protected the name of true "knighthood;" a badge of honor that called knights to a higher standard and prevented them from misusing their powers.

Teens today also need a similar badge of honor. They need to be made aware of the royal bloodline they've descended from. They need a code that calls them to a higher standard of conduct. But more important, it must be a code that inspires them to know their noble heritage and the King they serve. Teens desperately need such a code of honor today. They need an identity that calls them to idealistically stand for principles and passionately protect innocent people.

I repeat this saying often: *Kids can do heroic things, but they need heroic things to do.* No matter how outwardly weak, awkward, and unappealing teens may appear, they are internally wired for the electricity of noble deeds to light them up inside. But this wiring gets easily crossed in a culture that has lost its badge of honor. It's a culture where disrespect and brutality seem to be the current standard.

How Adults Have Set the Stage for Brutality

How Adults Have Set the Stage for Brutality

School hallways are daunting places for many teens. They are places where you can be checked out, laughed at, put down, and roughed up—all in one short three-minute stroll between classes. And if you report the abuse to a teacher, much worse may happen at another unexpected time and place.

Giants who misuse their strength are becoming more common in the teen world today. Theirs is a culture of Four B Davids and Goliaths, but the little guys are not always the good guys and they don't use slingshots anymore. To many teens—especially boys—the Four Bs seem to have lost any connection to desirable ends that relieve pain. For growing numbers, the game has completely changed from legitimately winning in the competitive arenas like school, sports, jobs, and relationships to getting the immediate rush, the sensual pleasures of money, sex, power, and fame (or infamy) any way possible. Some kids skip the hassle of competing fairly and squarely in the Four B arenas when brutality, cheating, stealing, and manipulating the media can also work the same toward self-serving ends. It's what I call "WWE ethics" (World Wrestling Entertainment™).

Ethic #1: Might is right.

Ethic #2: The end justifies the means.

In WWE, brutality is beautiful as long as it gets you to your goal. Pleasure becomes a learned perversion called "pain-watching." I'm completely at a loss to understand any kind of scoring system, if there is one. It's an absolutely upside-down morality. The rules of the ring blur good guys and bad guys; they change back and forth. It's a chaotic free-for-all duel of survival of the cruelest. If there is any vague purpose behind the nonsense, I think it is this: Be as brutal and mean as you can be on your way to the top, because once you get there—even if you're hated, at least you'll matter.

Baby Boomers, however, at least have a vague soul-memory of a definite rule book of natural morality, right and wrong, good and bad. We still see the world through the eyes of a moral referee who stands above every competitive arena, who upholds unchanging rules, who ultimately crowns the true champions—not the ones who muscle or cheat their way to the apparent top. We believe it's not whether you win or lose, but how you play the game.

Do we Baby Boomers understand that our kids are growing up with terribly blurred moral lenses? For many of our kids the idea of a moral referee (or any authority figure) is an impotent circus ringleader who runs around scolding the fighters but who is constantly frustrated because he can't control them. Ultimately his job is done when he lifts the hand of the person standing at the end.

What has caused such a drastic change in the nature of the game? I have a simple story that may explain how we helped build the arena for the

WWE ethics. Our ignorance is setting the stage for the moral handicaps our children now must live with. The ancient code of ethics has been locked away. And it is our duty to bring it back.

The New Morality Pills

Through all recorded history there has always been a bottle of pills called "Morality: What's Good for You."

The instructions on the pill bottle have always read: "Take the medicine and you'll become happy, healthy, and free."

There have always been plenty of pills for everybody because God made the ingredients naturally. And the Morality Pills have always been available free of charge. When we were young kids most of the medicine in the Morality Pill bottle was still being made with God's good, old-fashioned, natural ingredients of truth, goodness, justice, and mercy. The recipe has never changed because the basic nature and needs of people haven't changed. People have always needed to learn the same basic things about what is good and true and best to make us happy, healthy, and free. The same morality medicine has been passed down from generation to generation and it has always worked pretty well. What was good for great, great, great, great grandpa is good for you and me. The size and shape of the pills may have changed over the years, but the basic ingredients didn't change.

But during the last generation some social scientists started experimenting with the Morality Pills. They thought they could do a better job making up ingredients than God did. So they started inventing new Morality Pills that could numb pain and make people real happy really fast. The new medicine gave people a rush and made them feel powerful and in control. Mainly people liked the pills because it made them feel good immediately. So they demanded more and more of them to be made. Most of the new manmade ingredients in the Morality Pills were called *legislation,* or manmade laws. Another ingredient was called—*political correctness* (a big word that means popularity). Basically, the ingredients were no longer natural— and they became overly abundant. The problem with the experiment was that the scientists weren't really sure how long people's happiness would last, or what the side effects would be. The new pills were always changing. But the scientists also stood to make a lot of money (and make themselves a lot more happy) when they could control the factories that made the ingredients for these new Morality Pills. The main factories were in places called

Media, Education, Politics, and Business.

Then problems started happening. The new Morality Pills began having harmful and unpredictable side effects. Instead of people being happy and healthy, they eventually became sadder and sicker. People became numb. They could hurt other people very badly and wouldn't feel a thing. People were getting nearsighted and couldn't see beyond what might happen beyond their own noses. They could step on other people's toes and were totally deaf to the cries of pain. Instead of people becoming free (like the label on the Morality Pill bottle still said) they seemed to feel more like prisoners of fear and bad habits. Instead of feeling more alive, they started feeling like robots, impulsively doing everything that wacky scientists everywhere would tell them was good.

Because the experiment was backfiring, the scientists became worried that people would go back to their old natural morality medicine that worked. Their experts in Media, Education, Politics, and Business would stand to lose a lot of money and power! So they began going to court to make it illegal to talk about the old-fashioned, natural Morality Pills. No one was even allowed to say that someone was "right" or someone was "wrong," because those were definitely two key ingredients of the old-fashioned pills. The scientists would try to make it illegal to even mention the Name of the Maker of the old-fashioned pills (God). They knew that his pills were free, and that the bottle was always available. And deep down, many of them knew God's natural Morality Pills really did work better. But at least if they could keep people unaware of them, they would keep their jobs in their powerful new morality factories.

Eventually the scientists put most of their focus on the Education factory. They schemed and planned that if they could just train kids how to use the false formula called subjectivism that kids could learn to become inventors of their very own Morality Pills. But the problem was that *subjectivism* had no real ingredients of *goodness,* but only gave kids a very addictive ingredient called *power.* Then, with so many new Morality Pills making kids compete for power, the scientists stayed very, very busy making and selling their ingredients of legislation. They were so busy all the factories eventually joined into one big factory called government.

But many of the common people still remembered and went back to the good, old-fashioned pills anyway. The bottle still said, "Morality: What's Good for You." The instructions on the bottle still read, "Take the medicine and you'll become happy, healthy, and free." The public world seemed a lot less happy, healthy and free. It took courage for common folks to take God's natural medicine those days. It took much love to share the natural goodness with others. But as more and more brave souls partook, they indeed became happy, healthy, and free. Their communities became more peaceful and prosperous than they had ever known before.

Obviously, the story is fantasy. There are no mad moral scientists—at least not self-aware, moral scientists. But there are so-called experts in the Four B arenas who carry much clout over what constitutes right and wrong through legislation. These "experts" are skeptical and cynical about there being a "Moral Referee" and they seek to remove objective moral truth, or the "Old Morality Pills," from influencing the public arena.

Deep passion for reality and truth are hardwired into the teenage heart. Teens seem ever ready to champion a good cause. But if they are refused the opportunity to face valiant challenges to conquer their dreams for doing great things, idealism and passion sour into doubt. Skepticism is a mutiny of doubt in the soul. It overthrows one's sense of higher purpose. Skepticism eventually gives way to cynicism, the belief in unbelief, and the restriction of the love-flow through the heart. Courage, however, is the good fight of faith and resists cynicism and unbelief and frees the soul to sacrificially love others.

I believe there is still hope for brutal youth, because of God and his wonderful design of their souls. They can be reborn to know their royal and noble heritage. They can be redirected to know their Maker by following his wonderful ways—the ways of mercy, justice, goodness, and truth. God's ways disarm the power of pain, fear, disappointment, and deception that misdirect young souls and arm their hearts with hate. Good is more powerful than evil. And we must pray and fight that God's will be done on earth even as it is in heaven. We must not ever throw in the towel. We must believe that God's might can make all things right again—that his ways work best to bring about the greatest happiness, health, and freedom

Kids can be brutal to other kids. And our adult world has come up with a gazillion Band-Aids—everything from video and poster campaigns about harassment to school police and metal detectors. We fly over their war zone and drop our character education packages without knowing for sure where our messages land. Mostly it's on deaf ears. And really, why should they believe us? Why would our "propaganda" carry more weight than the messages they hear from their peers?

Search Institute's study on teen values also revealed that only 27 percent of teens see their parents and other adults as modeling positive and responsible behaviors, compared to 60 percent saying their best friends were good models of responsible behavior (The subjectivism scandal must be working!) I've seen teen eyes glaze over as we repeat all our "opinions." The words are not new to them. Before we send more messages—the shoulds and should-nots—we need to rebuild the right frame of reference. They need to understand both the new and old views of how the "Morality Pills" are made. And they need to be equipped with the mental "laboratories" of proper logic to put both formulas to the tests of real science. They need the ABCs of critical thinking to answer the question of "What's Good for Them to Do?" But few, if any of these approaches are really available to reach the hearts of youth in the heart of youth culture—public schools. This is the place of multiple moralities, and the one with the most power wins.

The Tyranny of Terrorists and Schoolyard Bullies

Jason was an eighth-grade bully in middle school. He was only slightly bigger than the other boys, but his bad attitude made him a tyrannous giant in school. Jason had a terrible record of coercing students, conflicting with teachers, then getting kicked out. It was a dreaded day if he showed up on your new class list. The hallways were Jason's turf, and he had plenty of unruly serfs in his playground kingdom at school. But I remember the day when a teary-eyed teacher in a staff meeting shared a story of how she saw Jason's heart disarmed.

Jason's desk was stuck in the back corner of the classroom at a safe distance from other kids. His nearest neighbor was Kenny, a boy confined to a wheelchair due to a congenital disability. Kenny was small for his age, soft-spoken and kindhearted. But he was also a very hard worker, wheeling himself from class to class and bouncing back from several medical crises. On occasion Jason had to pair up for an assignment. It was convenient that Kenny was closest because he was the only kid willing to be Jason's partner anyway. The stage was set for something profound hidden in the unlikely pairing of bully and broken kid.

Late in the year, Kenny was out of school for several weeks to have his fourth major surgery in his thirteen years of life. That's when his middle school classmates adopted him as their sparrow kid. Among other service events, the students did a coin drive to help raise funds for Kenny's recovery. Every day at the beginning of class, a student leader would carry the coin container to the office to have the money accounted for.

On the last day of the drive, however, the teacher made a final call. Just then Jason came forward. From the back of the room he bumped through rows of desks, making his way to the front of class. The other students sat in silent shock, seeing Jason's humongous coin jar and then witnessing the known bully empty it into Kenny's container. The choked-up teacher described the ennobled look on Jason's face when he returned to his desk amongst the cheers and applause of his classmates. Perhaps for the first time, he was recognized and respected by his peers for doing something heroically good.

Unless their hearts are disarmed like Jason's was, bullies will bully. It makes no difference if they are bullies in the hallway, gang-bangers in the hood, or terrorists around the globe. All tyrants, young or old, use their power like giants to take from instead of give to other people. Their goal is to self-protect, not self-sacrifice. Their hearts beat with alternating intent to put others down and put themselves up. And they never admit that their ruthlessness is unprovoked—I've had many of them in my office over the years. It's amazing the blame and excuses you can hear, and they actually believe themselves! Power blunts the conscience of the callous and dulls self-awareness.

Benjamin Netanyahu, former prime minister of Israel, remarked in a speech about how terrorists justify their cruel acts.

The terrorists say, "You're terrorists because you kill civilians too. America, Britain, Israel—all are terrorist states." We must harden ourselves against this amoral and debilitating charge. Terrorism is not defined by the identity of its perpetrator. Nor is it defined by the cause, real or imagined, that its perpetrators espouse. Terrorism is defined by one thing and one thing alone. It is defined by the nature of the act. Terrorists systematically and deliberately attack the innocent. That is a very different thing from the unintentional civilian casualties that often accompany legitimate acts of war.

I suspect that these older tyrants began as young tyrants, who were victimized by lies, fears, and wounds early on. Then their hearts became hardened. At some point they were wounded, weakened, and overpowered by the spirit of hate and revenge. Dameon called it "payback time." He was tempted by it, as we all are at some level. But revenge is perverted justice and totally self-indulgent. It returns evil for evil. A tender heart gets wounded; the wounds are not taken care of, become infected, fester, and swell with bitter thoughts. Eventually the heart explodes with rage. But human rage knows no balance—it always creates more victims and does more damage than good.

True justice is always balanced by mercy, never metes a greater measure of pain than necessary to bring about a greater good. Justice creates perfect equilibrium in a soul to make decisions based on truth and not just emotion. It does this by steadily draining and relieving pain in the pathway of mercy. Kindness can turn a raging river of revenge into a restorative flow of help for another. The biblical "code of chivalry" sets an extremely high standard for resisting personal vindication. "If your enemies are hungry, give them food to eat. If they are thirsty, give them water to drink" (Prov. 25:21–22, NLT).

Tyrants know no stillness or peace. They privately declare war on everyone who doesn't see things their way or cater to their cravings for control. For them, "might is right." Power is their guiding principle. In the words of the infamous tyrant Adolf Hitler, "Power is the supreme law." But I believe a tyrant's hunger for power is connected to another misguided end—personal glory. Tyrants are essentially glory seekers. For them power is the supreme cause-and-effect law for getting glory. To be glorified means to get attention—to be honored, respected, or admired by someone. In the deepest sense—to be feared.

Tyrants long for fame, even if it is infamy. The media is their stage. In the classroom, it may be as innocuous as a name on the chalkboard. For international terrorists, it's CNN. As the platitude puts it, "Power corrupts. Absolute power corrupts absolutely." But I believe it is a personal pursuit of glory that corrupts the power people possess—and terrorists love to show off the damage they do to any person in their path. No person is exempt from glory seeking. As Saint Augustine wrote in A.D. 415, "The desire for fame tempts even noble minds."

But the glory bullies get only a drug that numbs a deeper pain they feel—fear. They fear people. They fear retribution. Fear is really their dictator. It controls them no matter how hard they try to control it. As the ancient eastern proverb says, "Dictators ride to and fro on tigers from which they dare not dismount."

Fears can become a quicksand pit in all of us. It is a place of desperation for control. It haunts us all and pulls us to want power to some degree. Fear can drive us to two extremes. One path is a desire to control everything, to be hyper-vigilant. The other is perhaps worse. It is to do nothing, to drown in our circumstances. It's a cowardly state of the soul called a victim mentality. Those with a victim mentality fail to accept any responsibility.

But God equipped each soul with a wonderful way to overcome fear. The brawn of courage can lift our souls above threats and fears. The quote of Jesus inscribed in the lobby of the Central Intelligence Agency in Langley, Virginia, says, "And ye shall know the truth, and the truth shall make you free." Our Rock is God. And real inner brawn—Courage—clings to his unchanging truth and sets our souls free from the quicksand of fear. God is in control and we need not fear the worst bully!

Oliver Wendell Holmes said, "Truth is tough." Truth is strong enough to anchor the weight of our soul's trust. Courage reaches out and holds onto truth in the face of fear and sets our hearts free to do heroic things!

Setting the Stage for Chivalry

Behind the scenes over the past few seasons, the University of Washington Huskies football team has set the stage for chivalry. Each year they have adopted a young boy with cancer, a sparrow, through our Sparrow Clubs organization. An article in the *Seattle Post Intelligencer* quoted quarterback Marques Tuiasosopo when he said, "It wasn't something we had to do [helping a sick kid]—it was something we wanted to do. Football isn't life. If it becomes your life, you need to step back and get things in line. There are a lot of things out there that are more important." I believe "getting things in line" refers to putting love into the equation of everything we do and using one's strength for more noble purposes than simply beating opponents. And, by the way, doing the chivalrous service project did not weaken the team's competitive edge on the field—they won the Rose Bowl Championship that year. Other college programs are beginning to use this model to build a more noble and giving spirit into their teams.

Modern society has devalued the code of chivalry and reduces teens to such minor roles they have no hope of doing heroic things. But every teen must know they have a badge of courage and honor stamped on their hearts by the King. They have been called to the high purpose of defending justice in his domain of truth. But how do we set the stage for teens to become players in this new, more heroic drama? They need a true drama, a script that invites them to act in this noble role—much different from the one their world has handed them.

Perhaps the code of chivalry would work. Before young men were dubbed into knighthood they had to serve as pages and then squires. They were armor bearers and apprentices for noble knights, who mentored them in the ways of virtue and valor. Squires even went to the battlefields to fight alongside their knights. After squires proved to be worthy warriors, their lord or king dubbed them into knighthood, too. Those early years of training were vital in painting the dream of future heroism in the hearts of squires and pages.

Teens today need the mentorship of older knights who hold to a code of chivalry. They need the picture of heroism painted in their dreams. They need to be taught bravery, honor, courtesy, respect, generosity, protection of the weak, and also fairness towards their enemies. They need an inner training camp to help them build up their moral muscle fibers of resolve and resilience. And they need special skills that help them make a difference in the lives of others.

The Mentorship of a Retired Knight

I believe in angels and heroes—and knights in shining armor. They are God's special lifters who unexpectedly and without fanfare enter our world and lighten our loads. I believe God sent an angel into my life in late August of 1992. Just after Michael got out of the hospital for his bone-marrow transplant, I met Shin Matsutani. I needed to report back to work at Kamiakin Junior High the day Michael was released to go home from the hospital. Michael, however, wasn't medically out of the woods yet. Life was difficult. I was buried under heavy responsibilities at school as the athletic director, activities director, leadership teacher, regular PE teacher, adaptive PE teacher, and assistant football coach—along with my full plate at home. Needless to say, I didn't want to be at school. But at the same time, it could have been a lot worse. I couldn't help but count my blessings. My son was alive! My reasons to complain were all but nonexistent.

By chance, a small-statured, humble, and quiet Japanese man named Shin dropped by my office at school. He was new to the community and came by to see if I needed to hire any football coaches. He was just looking for some work to keep him busy. I learned that Shin had taught in Los

Angeles City Schools for twenty-five years. He was a master PE teacher, department head, and coach before he retired and moved to the Seattle area. From his letters of recommendation and resume I realized that Shin was a "dollar bill" interviewing to a "dime." His skills and experience far surpassed mine! One of his references revealed his nickname, "Little General." He was a man who aspired to be what he taught—a man of steel and velvet, tough and tender. He had that rare combination that commanded both respectful fear and admirable love from his students. Later on I heard there were only two people who could walk down Wilmington Boulevard at midnight on Saturday and the gang shooting would stop. Coach Matsutani was one of them. He was a knight with the shining armor of respect.

I didn't have any coaching job openings. But I briefly shared with Shin what was on my plate and was happy to offer him my assistant football position. But later that same day, after taking time to contemplate my offer, Shin came back with his own four-point, clearly and concisely articulated offer:

1. He would volunteer as my assistant coach. He would give me his time.

2. He would not accept pay. If we paid him he would give the money to me.

3. He would shadow me as long as it took to learn my job.

4. He would be my exclusive substitute at school; if ever there were an urgent need for me at home, I would go. Shin would come.

Four months earlier a hero named Dameon had come into my same office and stunned me. Shin must have been an angel—a miraculous and mysterious visitor who came and lightened my load. He was a hero to me too. He is a man who has grown to become my mentor and close friend ever since. We met many Saturday mornings for coffee—I'd call them "chalk-less" talks—when he shared his code of chivalry. One of the many lessons my mentor Shin taught me was that good teachers really must be coaches at heart. Did you know there is a difference? He said that teaching fills the mind with truth, but coaching trains the will to obey. Coaching gets kids to do right things right. When truth is obeyed, a person's heart-gifts are set free. That's when kids find their wings, and the winds of adversity only lift them higher.

I learned from Shin that parents are teachers and must be coaches, too. Perhaps they are the most important coaches in the world. I think we'd all do well to have a coach like Shin—older knights who mentor and discipline us and hold us accountable to act on what we ought to do, the things that help us find our wings.

Shin has moved back to Los Angeles now, where he takes care of his elderly relatives and church members who need assistance. He is steel and velvet. Heroes seem to put a halt to bad things. And I bet the shooting still stops for Shin on Wilmington Boulevard.

Lifters and Leaners

Courage exercises our strength to become burden "lifters" and not "leaners." There is a wonderful poem by Ella Wheeler Wilcox that captures the spirit of what it means to be a lifter in life. It's called "Two Kinds of People."

> There are two kinds of people on earth today,
> Just two kinds of people, no more, I say,
> Not the good and the bad, for 'tis well understood
> The good are half bad and the bad are half good.
>
> Not the happy and sad, for the swift flying years
> Bring each man his laughter and each man his tears.
> Not the rich and the poor, for to count a man's wealth
> You must first know the state of his conscience and health.
>
> Not the humble and proud, for in life's busy span
> Who puts on vain airs is not counted a man.
> No! The two kinds of people on earth I mean
> Are the people who lift, and the people who lean.
>
> Wherever you go you will find the world's masses
> Are divided in just these two classes.
> And, strangely enough, you will find too, I wean,
> There is only one lifter to twenty who lean.
>
> This one question I ask. Are you easing the load
> Of overtaxed lifters who toil down the road?
> Or are you a leaner who lets others bear
> Your portion of worry and labor and care?

I'm reminded of the opening lines of Scott Peck's classic book, *The Road*

Less Traveled: "Life is difficult. This is a great truth, one of the greatest truths. It is a great truth because once we truly see this truth, we transcend it."

Everyone on earth has a boatload of responsibilities and burdens to carry throughout life. This is a simple reality. I believe there are three types of *leaners* that we find in the world: lazies, cons, and bullies.

Lazies are weaker forms of tyrants, but tyrants still. They use the *injustice of irresponsibility* to place burdens on others. They don't intimidate, they manipulate. They presume their loads should not be carried by themselves. They dodge discomfort. They are pain avoiders who fail to see their own difficulties as their own responsibilities first. The lazy teen looks for every angle and excuse not to extend him or herself for others. They use their skills to get out of doing work, to bum money, and to find the path of least resistance.

Cons are cheaters. They use the *injustice of bribery* to exploit the rules and gain from another person's unfair loss. They use their intelligence, position, money, and image to manipulate systems and wrongly use the trust of people. They steal opportunities and rights of others and make competition unfair. It's becoming more common to hear of white-collar crime, of CEOs and corporate executives who personally leverage their position of trust and load up their pockets with company profits—leaving the investors to carry the burden.

Bullies use the *injustice of brutality* to intimidate, threaten, and force people to do what they want. They are essentially criminals who must be overcome with the greater good of resolve. I admire the people of Israel who live in the face of terrorist threats daily. The Jews have endured brutalities for thousands of years. And even though the Israeli government is known for its swift and sure use of force to protect her citizens, the backbone of Israel's fight against terrorism is not their weapons but the strong will of the common people. They simply refuse to shrink back in fear. They insist on maintaining a mindset and lifestyle of freedom and joy despite the cowardly attacks of terrorists on their innocent. From teens in schools that feel unsafe, to adults in a nation now threatened by terrorist acts, we would do well to learn from the Israeli attitude. We must all cling to justice and stand strong in the hope of God's protection or vindication.

Heroes, in contrast to lazies, cons, and bullies, are *lifters* and people of *inner brawn.* They are inwardly tough enough to face the fact that life is difficult. They carry their own burden of responsibility. They play fair, don't cheat, and if they do fail, they try to make up for it in an honorable way. They stand up for people and principles. They are givers who are sometimes outwardly Four B weak, but always inwardly Four C strong. And they use whatever Four B strengths they have to be burden-bearers and to build others up.

On the last day of school one year Shin was confronted in his office by three teens and eight bullets in the cylinder of a gun. They pointed it at him for being "too hard" and "not fair" as a teacher. His calculating thoughts were, "I was strict and fair. If I'm going to die for that, go ahead and pull the trigger." After the ordeal was over, he said, "I was at peace because I had a good cause to die." In another gun incident, though, he said he was afraid. A gang-banger from another neighborhood entered the school lunchroom, pointing a revolver at the cowering crowd of kids. Shin pushed his way through the crowd to find the pistol pointed at his face. The threat seemed so senseless. *I'm afraid because I have no cause,* he thought.

I think Shin's cause was just stepping in front of the gun. Who knows what might have happened if he didn't. Heroes are lifters—heroes are shields, too. A girl in his next class said, "Mr. Matsutani, if something happened to you my brains would starve." I believe he would tell you today that his inner strength comes from his convictions to trust and obey God and to stand for good causes.

The Inner Training Camp

In my training to become a physical education teacher and coach at the University of Washington, I earned a degree in kinesiology—the study of the human body and movement. I learned that physical power has two components: muscle strength and muscle endurance. Strength is the ability to move or overcome the resistance of an opposing force. Endurance is the capacity for muscles to sustain work over a longer period of time.

The Bible says, "Physical exercise has some value, but spiritual exercise is much more important, for it promises a reward in both this life and the next" (1Tim. 4:8, NLT). The soul needs practice resisting or pushing away wrong things and pulling for what's right and good. Teens need training to build inner brawn to pull for the rights of others and the principles of God's goodness.

No matter what sports young people play, to become competitive giants they must adhere to certain principles of training. I believe these same principles that operate in the physical realm also fully translate into conditioning the soul. In physical muscle training, the opposing force we must overcome is gravitational pull. In moral training, the opposing force is often *"gratifica-tional" pull*—the weight of our own wants, appetites, and immediate desires. The end result is an increased confidence and capacity to overcome greater challenges. The end reward of good work always makes the struggle worth-while. Building inner brawn brings us through the same process that a good training program does. Keeping our courage in a growth mode requires regu-lar effort, increasing challenges, and the encouragement of future victory.

I taught advanced training and conditioning and coached at Omak High School for nearly ten years. I tried to create an uplifting, hard-working, and competitive environment in my weight-training classes. I had several sayings painted on the weight-room walls. One quote from an unknown source was painted in especially big, bold letters that said, "The greatest reward for all my toil is not what I get for it, but rather what I become by it."

The point of this quote was to weave an important theme into all the work my students did in class—striving for the inner win is more important than getting the outer win. Overcoming weaknesses in faith and lack of excellence are the bigger wins in life. But the scoreboard always has a way of catching up to the soul. Inner victory precipitates outer wins too. The Four C roots cause the Four B fruits to grow. And even though I had a wall of fame where I posted records and top ranking scores for everyone to applaud, the quote was to remind them constantly of this truth, to inspire them in the great challenge of building inner fortitude or moral strength. The focus was turning competition inward. Real success is not a Four B goal they outward-ly attain, but becoming a person of strong faith and excellence within. In that context, the spirit of external competition against other "becomers" is likened to the process of iron sharpening iron—we use one another's strength and skill to sharpen the edge of our own capacities. By building moral resolve and resilience we can learn to act justly in the world.

Resolve is the faith power to pull us toward truth and goodness. It resists and pushes away evil and fear. Resolve is the practice of striving for greater goods that are above and beyond our immediate comforts. High purposes are like heavy weights: the greater they are the more opposing force we often feel. Heavy weight lifting requires a fixed focus. Through my own soul's regimen, I have come to experience that God's promises provide the best focus. "I can do all things in him who strengthens me" (Phil. 4:13, RSV).

Resolve also focuses on truth and arm wrestles fear to the ground. It gains power from a mind that is made up. It bows to the belief that God's strength will make all things right in the end. It takes moral muscle fiber, guts, and intestinal fortitude to regularly apply our hearts, heads, and hands to real problems. It keeps us leaning forward into the cold north winds of major adversity. Resolve confronts problems head on in the face of future pain. Resolve just does it! It helps us to face our fear of failure and overcome personal challenges that would be more comfortably avoided. Resolve is rooted in belief that failures are only stepping-stones to success.

Resilience is our capacity to endure hurts, tolerate pain, and bounce back from blows of discouragement. Soul resilience is built by working on forgiving and being forbearing towards others. Our souls, like muscles, can be stressed with long, grueling bouts of difficulty. But untrained human hearts, without a higher purpose, typically take the easy route. They look for excuses to be lazy. They blame somebody else out of bitterness and resentment. They get scarred, hardened, and desensitized like a callus.

Well-exercised, resilient souls, on the other hand, are flexible. They bend under pressure but do not snap. They get stretched and bounce back to good form because they've been properly trained. They are still sensitive to the needs of others despite insensitivity towards them.

Forbearance is a form of resilience that means to forgive people in advance of their offense or annoyance. Forgiveness is the exercise I call "restling." Forgiving is like a soul-based wrestling match. Our ego wrestles against giving up what we feel we deserve. We wrestle with the spirit of revenge. We struggle against injustices done to us. It is "grace under pressure." Our rights are violated. Our pride is stepped on. But again, the truth is anchored in what God and his justice deserve, not what we think we deserve. We rest-le by resting our case in God's hands for ultimate justice and his mercy to win out.

The Specialized Skill of Encouragement

I did an experiment one time with my weight-lifting class at Omak High School. It revealed the concrete results of what lifting others up can do. Before class, I chose two athletes, Gustavo and Ben, who had equal scores in the bench press—both could lift eight repetitions with 185 pounds. I asked the two if they'd like to participate in an experiment, but I didn't tell them the details in advance. Both agreed, and I isolated them outside the weight room while thirty of their classmates waited inside. In the weight room I explained the details of the lesson to the rest of the class.

I told the class that we were going to do an experiment with Gus and Ben, who could both lift the same amount of weight. I told them that we were going to see if encouragement gets real results, to see if having a team behind you really makes a difference. Here's how the experiment worked. The first athlete would come in and I would tell him to get on the bench press and lift 185 pounds as many times as he possibly could. I would count. The class was to remain dead silent, not saying a word. We agreed to choose Gustavo to be the non-encouraged lifter, because he was always so emotionally "fired up" on his own anyway, we thought it would make a better test.

Then I told the class that after Gustavo was finished, we would invite Ben in and instruct him to do the same thing. We would get behind Ben, however, with every bit of verbal encouragement and cheering we could muster. I told them encouragement had three components:

1. Use his name—encouragement must be personal.
2. Believe he can win—encouragement is born in the heart.
3. Say it positively and powerfully—"You can do it, Ben!"

The fun began when Gustavo came into the weight room and I gave him the basic instructions. He was shaking with excitement just to have people watching him bench press. He started and grunted and lifted his way in silence to a personal record of ten reps! Gus did a great job!

But then came stoic-natured Ben. After I gave him the instructions the class exploded with enthusiasm and encouragement. I mean, the walls were rattling! "Go, Ben! You can do it, Ben! Push it, Ben! You got it" … and Ben blew away his personal record … nine, ten, eleven, twelve, thirteen, fourteen! Ben's success was exhilarating for us all. Together we learned a powerful lesson that day—encouragement works! By our encouragement, we truly do share in one another's victories!

Encouragement is a tool for emotional weight lifters. It leverages the little effort we can muster to overcome big obstacles. Belief is the key. We must sell the idea to teens that we all share in some way with each other's successes or failures. There is no neutral ground. We are either for God's way of blessings and goodness winning out in another person's life or against it. This is the key to creating an encouraging atmosphere. It creates a learning climate that uplifts everyone involved. And as coaching great Vince Lombardi once said, "It's amazing what a team can accomplish when no one cares who gets the credit."

Protecting the Weak against Injustice

The motto on Thomas Jefferson's personal seal was "Rebellion to tyrants is obedience to God." The courageous founding fathers of our nation experienced firsthand the tyranny of a giant. The British government had exploited the God-endowed individual rights of common people. Our brave and wise forefathers knew there was only one power that was strong enough to lift their oppressed, fearful souls to resist the tyranny of giants. They knew that free people need a moral referee standing above any one person and masses of persons, holding all accountable to higher principles of truth and justice. This common knowledge was coined on our currency, "In God We Trust." Our nation was born under God, in freedom from fear and tyranny, and prospered greatly. We commonly agreed to bow our knees before God's power and laws. One fear consumed every other fear.

It would be an easy mistake to think that it was our courageous forefathers who upheld justice. In reality, the idea of God's truth and justice so inspired and lifted their hearts that they began to act justly, to overcome their fears, and to fight injustice. Our forefathers didn't establish justice—they clung to it, and justice established them! But today it's becoming more common to hear of tyranny, exploitation, and victimization in the worldly Four B arenas of media, politics, economics, and education.

Only in heaven is might purely right. Here on earth, the strong may be wrong. We must only exercise our might in right ways. But right builds might, and every citizen must be strong in his or her grasp of truth and justice and express it freely in every public forum.

Because public school teachers are on the government payroll, they are restricted in what they can say regarding God in their classes, but students are not restricted. They have a right to free speech in school. I have observed high school students stand before an assembly and admonish other students what is right to do and give glory to God. Their obedient courage makes me proud.

Pursuing the Hero of Their Dreams

You may recall the movie classic *Rocky*. It had a scene that especially resonated within me. Sylvester Stallone as Rocky Balboa was alone in his bedroom in his small stack house apartment. He was at a place of decision in his life. Would he accept the challenge to face the World Heavyweight Champion

Apollo Creed in a promoter's ploy? The plan was to give a Philadelphia unknown boxer the chance to enter the ring against the undefeated world champion in the bicentennial celebration in our nation;s city of birth. And there stood the uneducated, rough-cut, underemployed, semi-pro boxer, Rocky, who moonlit as a collector for a two-bit loan shark. Rocky was by chance chosen as Apollo's contender. Earlier on he'd been kicked out of the gym by Mick, the local trainer. He had just reciprocated by kicking Mick out his apartment after being labeled a loser and a "waste of life." Mick now wanted the job of training Rocky for the fight.

At one point, Rocky stood in front of his dresser mirror—facing himself as a grown man, fully realizing the disappointments, the waste his life had been, the failure he had become. And there, wedged in the frame of the mirror, his boyhood school photo stared at him. He picked up and gazed at the small picture of who he had been. There was no dialogue in the scene, just music in harmony with Rocky's heart and soul. Standing there, with the picture in his hand, Rocky seemed to be contrasting himself now as a man against his boyhood dreams of who he one day could be. Drawing from the innocent ideals of his boyhood Rocky projected himself into the possibility of a future comeback—comparing it against the shame and disgust of his present condition. Deep within, the passion was reawakened. The hero he once knew in a young boy's dream again came alive as one last chance.

In the prospect of near-certain defeat, Rocky chose to face the impossible challenge. In the spirit of forgiving himself, he gave himself a second chance. He rushed out to call Mick back—the man who had once rejected him was forgiven as well. It was not the outer man Rocky, that no-name loser who was kicked out of the gym as a bum, who decided to fight. No, I think it was a little boy's hero who answered the bell. The man of a boy's dreams was given new life—a taste of hope. Yes, he could still be the person he was meant to be. To pursue his vision and face humiliating defeat was worth more than to accept the failure of his inner man and face the loss of the noble warrior he could become.

I believe a most important challenge we have with teens today is to keep alive their dreams of doing something heroic. Again, young people are idealistic, passionate, and cause oriented. But if the cause is blocked, kids become cynical. Idealism and passion rebel against the dream. The problem is that we adults hold the key to most of the causes. We block the cause and the faith that our kids deeply need to put into action. By doing so, we ignorantly arm young hearts with skepticism—or neutered faith. It takes work on our part to give kids heroic things to do, things that make a real difference in the lives of other people.

Winston Churchill said, "To every man, somewhere in his lifetime, there comes a special moment when he is figuratively tapped on the shoulder and offered a chance to do a very special thing, unique to him and fitted to his talents. What a tragedy if that moment finds him unprepared, unqualified for the work which could be his finest hour."

Compassion and courage tap us all on the shoulder with impulses of love and bravery from time to time. If we fail to act when we are tapped, however, we can become numb to their touch. We parents and teachers may not realize that our teens are now being tapped by these same ideals. They sense them as impulses that awaken deep passions to be the person God made them to be. God uniquely wired teens to do special things. These things are perfectly suited to their talents. But they can only be discovered by meeting the needs of others, and they need us to point them in the right direction.

Lindsey Wilcox prepared herself to be a heroine by doing special things for other people in daily ways. Though her unique talents were buried beneath years of adversity and rejection, she clearly was a person of sacrificial love. Lindsey's final hour was her finest.

Chapter Five
Character: The Wealth of An Inner Bank Account

Chapter Five
Character: The Wealth of An Inner
Bank Account

All that glistens is not gold—Shakespeare

A t a national marketing conference a few years ago some eyebrow-raising statistics were shared about the spending patterns of the Echo Boomers. This segment of population includes over 70 million youth born between 1977 and 1994. It is the largest generation of kids since 78 million Baby Boomers hit the scene between 1946 and 1964. But there is one big difference between the Boomers and the Echo Boomers—teen consumerism.

Echoes have an estimated annual disposable income of $250 billion. Over half the kids between twelve and seventeen years old earn over fifty dollars per week for allowance. The average weekly income of thirteen to nineteen year olds is over $100. Forty-four percent have access to their parents' credit cards and 14 percent have one in their own name. They spent over $15 billion on recorded music in 1999 alone. And over 50 percent of trend-setting teens said if they had to choose between giving up food for a day or their music, they wouldn't eat! To say that media doesn't model and influence youth behavior is a bad joke. Eighty percent of female teenagers ranked advertising as very important in their buying decisions. Ninety percent read magazines. It's no surprise why marketing strategists and media moguls have targeted this young generation for their products and brands.

Jesus said, "No one can serve two masters. For you will hate one and love the other, or be devoted to one and despise the other. You cannot serve both God and money" (Matt. 6:24, NLT). A master is someone or something that has power or influence over us. Money is an acceptable servant, but a terrible tyrant as master. Money itself is not evil. But its place in our lives as the source of happiness is. Jesus said, "Wherever your treasure is, there your hearts and thoughts will also be" (Matt. 6:21, NLT).

It is written in the Bible, "The love of money is at the root of all kinds of evil" (1 Tim. 6:10, NLT). Money as master quickly coerces its slaves into injustices of vice, bribery, and other corruptions of the soul. Trust rooted in money instead of God is quite possibly the single most destructive power in our nation today. It is a power that drives surface living. And the statistics indicate that this dictator of materialism has a power grip on the souls of teens as well.

Nearly six hundred years ago Thomas á Kempis wrote a book titled *The Imitation of Christ*. Apart from the Bible, it is said to be the most widely read book in the world. Because neither God's truth nor human nature has changed, Kempis's words are as fresh and relevant as the day they were written. He had a Four B message as well when he wrote:

> But many persons weak and feeble in spirit pray in their hearts: "See how good a life such and such a man leads. See how rich he is, how mighty, how high in authority, how great in the sight of the people, and how fair and how beautiful in appearance!" If you give heed to everlasting goodness you will see that these worldly possessions and desires are of little worth, and that they are rather more irksome than pleasant, for they cannot be had or kept except by great labor and busyness of mind. The happiness of man does not depend on an abundance of worldly goods, because moderation is best.

Moderating Materialism

Material abundance is a good thing but not the best thing. Moderation keeps materialism at bay. It keeps the place for real happiness and inner abundance from being crowded out of teens' hearts.

Some close friends of our family spent two years on the mission field in Nicaragua. They taught school in a remote region. After they returned to the States, the wife described the first time she walked into a supermarket. She was so struck by the disparity in material goods in America compared to what they had in Nicaragua that she broke down and wept in the middle of the store. But she also explained another disparity. The richness of relationship, the abundance of community spirit, and the appreciation of the people they came to know and love made the grocery shelves in America seem empty.

Another friend grew up as a missionary kid in Pakistan. She explained how simple her life was compared to the complexities of teenage girls growing up in America today. She had virtually no choice in clothing. She wore one dress for school and had a pair of jeans for playing in. But when she describes those teen years, she speaks of the closeness and warmth of the people and culture she grew up in. There is no hint she feels cheated due to lack of material things.

The testimonies of many teens who have gone on short-term mission trips to Mexico typically highlight the same themes. They describe the outward poverty compared to what we have. The people, however, seemed happy and appreciative despite the lack of material things. These trips typically last only a few weeks, but the powerful impressions last a lifetime.

Moderation is a form of justice practiced inside the soul. It is having the balance of just enough stuff, no more or less, to do justice to our needs. With God as Master, money is kept in perspective and put in its proper place. It is a little thing, a tool to use wisely but not a treasure to hoard or strive after. Moderation is an antidote for the epidemic of materialism that robs the teen soul of real happiness. Real treasures are banked in heaven and deposited in hearts through relationship, not material things. Money may help teens numb or avoid pain. It may buy fun, music, material goods, and temporary pleasures. But money cannot buy lasting hope or happiness.

As George Bernard Shaw wrote, "There are two tragedies in life. One is to lose your heart's desire. The other is to gain it." To strive after and gain something that doesn't last or fails to meet your expectations brings emotional pain. Perhaps that is why teen suicide is so high in America. Kids are promised much but realize little when they pursue worldly goods. I know that my sense of plenty has more to do with the bounty inside me than the material abundance of things I own. Real, genuine happiness is gold that most often does not glisten on the surface of life. Real gold must be mined inside us. It is an inner bank account of soul richness.

The Treasure of True Happiness

Herds of deer live in the area surrounding our home. Happiness often approaches us the way deer sneak into our yard. If you go out looking for them they never come. But when you are productively occupied doing some other task like pulling weeds, the deer suddenly appear as if from nowhere. Happiness does not come to us instantly like a can of soda pop from a vending machine when we drop our coins in. It is best to simply make a space, a sanctuary for happiness, and simply carry on with our day-to-day duties of doing good things.

Another word for happiness is blessing. Pastor and author Ron Mehl shares what his mother once told him. "Don't just go looking for blessings in life. Be 'bless-able'!" That's motherly advice that I believe we should all take to heart. Didn't our heavenly Father design his creation in a very pre-dictable way to bless his creatures that live according to his laws? Isn't the call to "Be bless-able" just another way to restate the weight-room platitude: "The greatest reward for all my toil is not what I get for it, rather what I become by it."

Being bless-able means living intentionally or with good purpose. So how shall we intentionally live? If we meshed Mrs. Mehl's admonition with the call of moderation and alignment with God's moral law, we might come up with a mission statement that goes something like this: God is good and I realize that real happiness is a blessing from him. I will strive to live in such a way that my whole life becomes a prayer to receive his abundant goodness into my soul. Therefore I choose to bow my knees in thought, word, and deeds to simply do what God requires of me—to love mercy, to act justly, and to walk humbly with my God.

Walking with God in humility simply means to let him lead us. Obedience opens our hearts to unimaginable happiness. If God is leading us we will grow in our love for mercy. He takes our souls to places where we begin to clearly see the needs of others. Then He shows us what we can do about those needs. Acting justly is simply discerning and doing what we can best do to help.

Building a Wealth of Trust

Trust is the currency of all good relationships, safeguarded in one's bank account of character. Trust must be earned and learned. The "trust walk" is a simple exercise where teens can experience what a merciful, just, and humble walk feels like. I learned the activity at a youth camp years ago. I was matched up with another person and then blindfolded. My partner led me on a five-minute walk around the camp by holding my arm and giving me instructions like "Get ready to step over a log." As the blindfolded partner, I certainly sensed my need in the situation. My inability to see made me vulnerable to stumbling, wandering off course, and bumping into hard things. I felt doubtful, out of control, and humbled in my need for help. It took courage and humble obedience for me to trust him. My partner could have finished the course much faster had he not been burdened with my care. It took compassion and good character on his part to be trustworthy. But we both understood that this was not a competitive footrace. The "trust walk" had a higher end as a cooperative "heart race." The course was set in a different dimension of connecting my need with his higher purpose of bringing me along and winning my trust. In a self-centered world, finishing together and learning to walk in the cooperative dimension is a victory indeed.

The path of the Four Cs is a trust walk. Each of us must choose whom our trust partners will be. We must choose how merciful we will be as leaders and how much desire we pour into meeting the needs of others. Even though we may have merciful intentions, sometimes our help is not very helpful or justified. We must be aware of the justice of our actions, being careful not to exploit or enable the weaknesses of others.

Imagine the two of us sitting in a rowboat side by side; you have one oar and I have the other. Let's say that you are the coach, an experienced and stronger paddler who is trying to help me reach my destination across the lake. But what would happen if you do all the work and I decide to coast? We'd go in circles! The same is true if I did all the rowing and you decide to drift. Here's the point: Effective helping must match the desire and effort of the helped person to reach a mutual goal.

Compassionate people are lovers of mercy. They are trustworthy helpers. They have learned to see needs and understand other people's feelings. They know what vulnerability feels like and how painful it is to lack power in this Four B world. And they have learned to feel good about using their power to bring relief. The ability of the needy person to repay favors has nothing to do with the desire to help. Helping others is a reward in itself for the lover of mercy. It puts a different spin on a world filled with needy people. For the lover of mercy this means pure opportunity.

People of good character and courage act justly. They use their strengths to protect weaker people's rights and opportunities, helping them to become eventual helpers as well. Four B talents and treasures are less important than trustworthiness. When teens develop moral virtues with self-discipline, they mine and refine the gifts God gave them to become loving leaders and good helpers.

Good character is the capacity to use our inner properties properly in ways that build trust, happiness, and healthy relationships. Most teens today fail to see and appreciate the properties they have inside them. The Four Cs, as one model, is only an imperfect reflection of authentic goods inside them. The Four Cs are inner reflections of the Four Bs, the properties they know very well. Our hope is that we can begin to speak to the part of them that longs to love and be loved. That young people will learn to see their brawn, beauty, brains, and bank accounts more symbolically than desperately. And that they can exercise self-discipline for developing the real capacities of courage, compassion, conscience, and character that is within them.

Years ago, a particular senior class practiced their commencement ceremony in the high school gym. This was my teaching station so I watched a preview of that evening's graduation event. It was gratifying to reflect on the growth of these kids I had coached and taught over the previous six years. But the contrasting activities of two boys especially caught my attention that day. Ryan was at the podium practicing his valedictorian speech. He would attend an exclusive college on full scholarship to pursue his dream of becoming a doctor. The other boy, Jesse, was pleading with the administrator to allow him to participate in the ceremonies. Jesse had not yet fulfilled his requirements for graduation and he had relatives coming into town to watch. He was desperate to avoid the embarrassment and disappointment of his family.

I reflected back on the boys through the years, beginning as middle school students. Ryan was small, skinny, and a bit awkward. He loved basketball, but if teams were picked he would usually be drafted near to last. He was shy and unaffected by the crowd. But Ryan was also a self-disciplined, faithful worker who stuck to his goals.

Jesse, on the other hand, was a popular kid. He was physically gifted, matured early, and was naturally athletic. He was also bright, talented, and socially outgoing. Outwardly, Jesse had the edge over Ryan. But it seemed he relied on his talents to get himself out of doing work instead of learning to do better work. Jesse had many assets, but hustling his way out of predicaments had become a pattern. Little daily dodgings of self-discipline had a subtle way of eroding his hopes of future success. That day of graduation, I saw the culminating difference that small choices can make over time.

Misused Properties and
Misdirected Goals

Misused Properties and
Misdirected Goals

A teen's talents and treasures don't necessarily make them better or point them toward better things. These things merely magnify what they already are and get them to their goals faster. If teens cannot be happy with a little money, it's unlikely they'll be happy very long with a lot. If they have wrong priorities and goals before they have money, they'll likely do more damage with it. Until young people come to realize that the properties inside them (Four Cs) are more valuable than the material things they acquire outwardly, they will tend to squander their inner gifts by seeking pleasures that will continue leaving their hearts empty.

Ryan was certainly not perfect, and Jesse was not a bad kid, but their lives taught me that good goals and small choices do add up to make a tremendous difference. Having a goal of building good character helps teens to use their talents and treasures wisely.

When I was growing up, I enjoyed watching the television program *The Beverly Hillbillies.* You likely remember the show—or the reruns. The backwoods Clampett family, led by Uncle Jed, struck oil on their property; the Clampetts became instant multimillionaires and moved into a mansion in Beverly Hills. It was fun to imagine what it would be like stumbling into all that money. Instant wealth is something we are all tempted to dream about from time to time. But here was a family that came away unscathed by the incredible wealth they acquired. The humor of the hillbilly show was in the irony of a primitive family living in the lap of luxury like they were still in the backwoods. The swimming pool was a "cement pond" for all of Ellie May's critters. The billiard room housed the "fancy eatin' table." Pool cues were used as "pot passers" and on and on. The Clampetts were clueless about the real purposes or use of all their new luxuries. Granny even reminisced and longed to go back home because nothing seemed to work right. These newfangled things just weren't functional! The hillbillies were hilariously locked into their old lifestyles.

But the show had another subtle irony to it too. In contrast to the sophistication of Beverly Hills living the Clampetts brought with them the country freshness of simplicity, sincerity, and common sense—something rare and newfangled to Hollywood for sure! Episodes often featured con artists and crooks trying to scam the family out of their money. Their naiveté made them extra-vulnerable. But these displaced hillbillies, in all their lack of self-protection and inexperience in worldly ways, had some substantial things in their souls. Their simplicity and innocence gave them an edge of wisdom in human ways. Their contentment with who they were and lack of ambition and greed to get things they didn't need coated them like Teflon and made them resilient to the scam artists.

I wonder if the real irony of the hillbilly show was the contrast between who misused their properties most. Was it the Clampetts who misused what they outwardly owned or the crooks and high-society neighbors who showed by their envy and vice that they misused what they inwardly owned?

There is an intended use and purpose of our gifts. The use of our inner properties should reflect excellently on how we were made and why we are here. God is glorified in the good things we do. Internal justice is done when we properly use our properties. Our inner world becomes more orderly when we align with God's priorities and peace comes as a result.

Building the Inner Bank Account of Soul Prosperity

Every teen's soul was created to prosper. It was created to be bless-able and to usher blessings into the world. Their souls are designed by a good God to achieve worthy goals, to attain excellence, and to experience peace and happiness. Young souls were made to flourish in fruitfulness and grow toward completeness. A teen's inner bank account of assets or properties can and should be developed to prosper them greatly. Good character makes teens receptive to God's best in their life. It makes them trustworthy, reliable, and resourceful. It invites good relationships. A bank account of character is established by good choices. Teens with good character have happier lives, contribute to their culture, and overflow with the goodness of God.

The three tasks of character development are:

1. To patiently postpone pleasure with chastity.
2. To prudently pursue higher purposes with contemplation.
3. To make connections with one's perfections.

Patiently Postponing Pleasures with Chastity

Patiently Postponing Pleasures with Chastity

Sally and Tom were home-schooled teens who chose not to date. Though their feelings for each other were powerful, they kept their emotions at bay by avoiding physical affection. They didn't hug, kiss, or even hold hands. Over a few years time, they came to intimately know each other by writing letters and doing things with each other's families and friends. When I first listened to their story, I was struck with the sense of how unnecessarily old-fashioned it all sounded. But when I saw the video of their wedding day, my heart was won by their waiting. It seemed they had climbed to the summit of emotion by postponing their pleasure, and the view of it was majestic to me. And when they were interviewed a few years later, with one child in their arms and another on the way, the seed of romance they had protected in their courtship still seemed to flourish in their marriage.

Chastity is an old-fashioned word. In practice it creates a retaining wall inside the soul. It withstands the pressures and demands that our appetites and the world put upon us to pursue pleasure and avoid pain. Not all pain is bad and not all pleasure is good. Pain and pleasure are like talents and treasures, their goodness depends on how they promote growth and wellness in the soul, not how much or little we possess of them. Postponing pleasure and persevering through pain grow roots of character in the teen soul. Like Chinese bamboo trees, the deeper and stronger the root system, the more capable our teens will be in weathering storms and becoming productive in the future.

Chastity gives time and space to prepare for future delights that are greater than immediate pleasures. It postpones premature experiences and pleasures that we hunger for. At the same time it allows the thimble of desire more time to grow into a gallon-sized container ready for more abundant pleasures. Chastity reserves pages in our soul for a dramatic love story script to completely develop and beautifully unfold.

In his book *New Seeds of Contemplation,* Thomas Merton wrote:

> It should be accepted as a most elementary human and moral truth that no man can live a fully sane and decent life unless he is able to say "no" on occasion to his natural bodily appetites. No man

who simply eats and drinks whenever he feels like eating and drinking, who smokes whenever he feels the urge to light a cigarette, who gratifies his curiosity and sensuality whenever they are stimulated, can consider himself a free person. He has renounced his spiritual freedom and become the servant of bodily impulse. Therefore his mind and his will are not fully his own. They are under the power of his appetites. And through the medium of his appetites, they are under the control of those who gratify the appetites.

Teens who are controlled by sensual appetites have no more freedom than dogs on leashes. One end of the leash of impulse is tied to the appetite, the other is held by someone or something that controls the means of satisfying the appetite most immediately. Teens who are mastered by money instead of God cease to be fully human. Desire pulls them on the leash toward material pleasures. They are led like dogs by impulse for things. They have no real freedom because there is no room in their soul to be aware of other real options. They are made numb with fun, and held captive by the promise of more. Teenagers' impulses, appetites, and desires for immediate gratification make the soil of their hearts unready to sow the seeds of creative choice for doing good. Impulsiveness crowds out and clutters the place of prosperity within them. In order to expand teens' capacity for future happiness, a space must be cleared in their hearts and minds. But the soul that puts to good use the heart-gift of intention begins to reflect a divine nature and inner beauty.

Merton goes on to say, "You will never find inner solitude unless you make some conscious effort to deliver yourself from the desires and the cares and the attachments of an existence in time and in the world."

Teens tend to be impulsive reactors. Chastity is a moral virtue that cuts the leash of their impulses. It creates space for thoughtfulness, good intentions, and pure desires to grow in between their impulses and reactions. Delaying gratification is a tough thing to do. It burns. But it gives us freedom from the leash of our appetites. Teens need space inside their souls to learn about and seek the fulfillment of desires that are more precious than anything money can purchase.

Chastity also gives teens time for silence and solitude. I heard a story of an African expedition years ago. A team of adventurers from America had come to Africa bulging with all their supplies, so they went to a nearby village to hire some natives to help them carry their loads. For several days the team was frantic to stay on schedule and ambitiously reach their destination. The pace was fast. One morning at the end of the first week the team restlessly readied themselves to continue their journey. They started down the trail but soon realized the natives were not following them. The team leader anxiously rushed back to the camp and questioned the interpreter why the natives were delaying. The interpreter replied, "Kind sir, we must wait. For our souls have not yet caught up with our bodies."

Our teens' souls have not caught up with their bodies either. And we don't help. We are so anxious to keep our young natives from getting restless that we just keep them moving faster and faster. Lack of peace is only driving us all to a faster pace from it. Chastity and contemplation cause us to slow down and reconsider where our roots must grow to find it. We parents tend to allow ambitious and competitive agendas to dictate our life's journey as well. As E.B. White said in 1944, "Everything in life is somewhere else, and you get there in a car." In 2003 you get there with a computer. We foolishly seek speed and technology when we have lost our place in life. We have made little time for reflection—for being in one place long enough to put down roots. Until we do, our souls will never catch up to our bodies.

The media bombards youth with marketing mantras and floods their minds with impulses. Their resistance is repeatedly battered down to experience everything they can right now. Ronald Rolheiser gets to the heart of the issue in his profound book, *The Shattered Lantern,* when he wrote:

> But have we not always been restless? Are we not pilgrims on earth, built with hearts made for the infinite, caught up in very finite and limited lives? Should we be surprised that we are constantly tormented by the insufficiency of everything attainable? To be hopelessly restless proves little more than that we are alive, emotionally healthy, and normal. Has not God built us so that we are restless until we rest in God?

This is a restlessness that power-hungry people certainly seek to exploit in kids. Chastity protects the sanctuary in our hearts for God's best. It allows time for the soul to long for something wonderfully good and to be stretched enough to contain and appreciate it fully. Chastity is the daughter of patience. And patience is a tough mother! But she certainly has good and kind intentions.

Prudently Pursuing Higher Purposes with Contemplation

Prudently Pursuing Higher Purposes with Contemplation

I knew a professional athlete who had plenty of money to spend when he went into shopping malls. But he had a habit of leaving his wallet in the glove box of his car. That way, when he saw something he wanted, he'd be forced to walk back out to get his money. The walk helped him to quiet the emotional "noise" of the buying impulse in his heart so that he could contemplate the buying decision in his head. By the time he made it to the car his "wants" would wear off enough for him to make a wise decision based on his need.

Contemplation fills the time and space created by chastity with thoughtful listening. It is a vital part of prayer. It is perhaps the most important part, to develop our capacity to tune into the still, small voice of truth above all the stimulus and noise of the world. Prayer that invites God's blessing and real happiness is not simply a word formula to be compulsively parroted so that we can cash in or be more comfortable. Rather it is an invitation for God to make our thoughts and desires more conformable to his—which may require some soul-stretching patience.

Prudent people use reasonable foresight and carefully consider their direction and steps through life. They are careful to maximize the best opportunities and minimize needless risks. There are two basic things a prudent person understands; it's the difference between "real goods" and "feel goods." Real goods are higher purposes that really are good for us. We truly ought to seek and desire them whether we feel like it or not. God designed real goodness so that our attainment of real goods never unjustly steps on someone else's toes. It protects and prospers them instead.

Feel goods are things we immediately desire. They are low-hanging fruits and require little if any work to obtain. At first glance they may apparently seem good, but they may or may not be good for us in the end. Often they are rotten. Feel goods are self-indulgences that are gained at the expense of others.

Real goods are things that nourish and grow deep roots. They bear fruits of happiness, health, freedom, and even the Four Bs as we practice them. Natural moral law, the code of chivalry, the Ten Commandments, and the Beatitudes govern them as surely as the sun rules the day and the moon rules the night.

An especially popular myth today regarding human desire is the sexual preference myth. Some would lead kids to believe that "certain impulses" of desire suggest an absolute imprint on their soul that locks them into an "alternative lifestyle". But the true gift and beauty of having human properties is that we can learn to alter our appetites. To a degree, we can rewrite our own scripts of desire when they are traced from the patterns of truth. Objective truth and real goodness give us permanent forms to fit our desires into. We can conform our will to God's higher purposes, which we can't immediately see or feel. When we come to desire the real goods—either good things to be, do, or have—we will live happier, healthier, and more freely in them.

Good goals are a blueprint where right desires can be clearly framed in our minds. Good goals are always matters of choice, not chance or feelings. The role of a goal is to be a vehicle to carry us through necessary moments of displeasure and pain to a place of hope. By postponing immediate gratification we may not feel good in the moment, but we learn to feel good about our future. Goals are the framework for the bricks of good choices to build a large bank for happiness for our hearts. Discipline, effort, and cause-and-effect laws cement our choices brick by brick. When we are not guided by a firm commitment to a goal, we become wanderers and scavengers for whatever meager existence we can forage from our immediate environment. With a goal, we become more of what God intended us to be—his image-bearers in the world—purposefully creative and productively at work . Eventually we sense a real structure of good character is forming inside us. Good habits of attitude, knowledge, and skills create an inviting place for success, prosperity, and happiness to find a home.

Perfections as Connections

I think of Mother Teresa. I'm convinced that she was not poor in spirit or meek and humble out of powerless fear. No, outwardly she wore the cloak of poverty because inwardly she was given greater riches. Her inner abundance afforded her the luxury of outer poverty. Her purposeful pursuit of serving the "poorest of the poor" was not by helpless default. It was by wisest intention and lofty design. A way of great gain was structured into her life. She discovered a hidden treasure, a pearl of great price, and sold everything she possessed to purchase something most would see as disgusting. She was an opportunist who insightfully and fortunately stumbled into a better deal.

Happiness is a state of being, not a state of having. It is based on perfections not possessions. But there is a connection to our soul perfections that goes beyond the self. Being loved and being loving are essentially the two connections that bring our soul "delight." The inner bank account of delight has more to do with enlarging and perfecting our heart-vault than with having tangible possessions. But this inner bank is also a place for deposits and withdrawals, for giving and receiving love. It is a place of serving people.

The peak of human delight this side of heaven, I believe, is rooted in simple humility. It is coming to a place of fully realizing our need for God, yet discovering it as an unfolding opportunity to greatly please him. The greatest joy in life is not in simply being bless-able, but in finding our heavenly Father to be please-able. It is a life of connection in a vertical dimension. It is a rose deeply rooted and in full bloom. Tapping into the greatest source of love at the place of our deepest need and also expressing our love to the one who is most worthy of it. It is kneeling at the cross and standing to cast our crown. It is brokenness and joy at once.

The poor in spirit realize their need for God. They are set free from their independence from God. And in that realization, in the brokenness of an impoverishing moment, with their face in the dirt of life, the glimmer from a half-buried gem meets their inner eye. God's grace surprises us in the most humble places. Poverty is not a glorious end in itself. But external poverty releases us from the tyranny of materialism. We are free to become bond servants to hope and love.

Was Mother Teresa's vow of poverty an entirely selfless act? I would venture to say yes and no. Giving is a mystery. It is selfless intentionally yet self-fulfilling indirectly. Goodness always has a way of giving back. And this is the way of all good goals. The heart that is open to let go never fails to receive more.

Mother Teresa's acts of charity were acts of great wisdom as well. Wisdom is a tool with which we discern real value, hidden quality, and not-so-obvious solutions that are oh-so-simple. Wisdom helps us hear the whisper of deeper meaning and read the symbols of higher purpose in life.

Disarming the "It's All About Me Syndrome"

Disarming the "It's All About Me
Syndrome"

Impulses and appetites may block the capacity of kids to be intentional, but it's the "It's All About Me Syndrome" (IAAMS) that blocks most of their blessings. It blocks them because their self-improvements and properties have no connecting ends of relationship. Connecting our heart-gifts to benefit others keeps the flow of goodness fresh and alive in us. IAAMS is a deep-seated mistaken belief with tentacles into nearly every bitter heart, bad attitude, and misbehavior. IAAMS is a soul sickness that detaches teens from the reality that their lives are interwoven with many other lives. Relationally healthy kids connect their personal story to a drama much bigger than their own. But IAAMS is the nearsighted view that their personal views contain the entire picture. It's also known as *narcissism*—a disconnected condition of being overly self-interested and one that leads to self-indulgence. Our soul is a hollow vessel that must be attached to others in give-and-take relationships in order to be fulfilled and constantly refilled.

Every human relationship has a healthy pulse and flow of give-and-take. Like gentle waves rolling across the sea there is an upside and a downside in relationships. Sometimes we're burdened with needs that should open us to seeking help or receiving grace. While my needs are being met, I am also thinking about ways to give assistance to others. With IAAMS, however, there is no wave of give-and-take. There are only one-directional curves that encircle the self. The self-first direction is a common one for teens and two year olds who are learning independence but have not yet learned healthy interdependence. It is called *entitlement* or the "I deserve everything" attitude.

Learning a healthy give-and-take balance is a necessary part of growing up. We parents definitely feel the frustration of having a kid going through the "I want, I need" life stage. In my research, however, I came across a wonderful report by Dr. Lynne Namke titled, *YOU OWE ME—Children of Entitlement*. In her report she shared several reasons some teens seem to get stuck with this extreme entitlement or narcissistic mindset. They include:

Being traumatized by physical or verbal abuse as children,
Being deprived of basic needs and love,
High family stress or loss (due primarily to divorce),
Being materially indulged (often by parents who have divorced),

Being spoiled materially vs. emotional relationship with parents,
Having negative role modeling of a self-indulgent parent(s).

Teens who are stuck in entitlement have a warped sense of injustice. They have learned to be overly sensitive to their own whims. I recall one young man who unleashed a torrent of profanity at me for a simple correction I made of his behavior in the hallway. I didn't even know his name at the time, but later learned that this was a pattern. It never failed that his mom would wholeheartedly take his side for being "picked on" by teachers. Proverbs 9:7 says, "Anyone who rebukes a mocker will get a smart retort. Anyone who rebukes the wicked will get hurt" (NLT). To kids like this, real justice feels like injustice. They burn with resentment. "That's not fair" is often the sincere but ridiculous heart cry of narcissistic teens. For an accurate sense of justice to be restored inside them they need to experience clarifying contrasts. They must get outside themselves and empathize with the needs of other people who are legitimately broken, yet who still maintain a grateful spirit in the midst of it. They need to appreciate the chances they've been given. As parents we must learn how to use the "Shin approach"—be steel and velvet. As a parent it's tough to be both strict and also fair. It's especially hard work if we were indulged as kids.

The other self-centered disconnected curve that some teens get stuck into is on the uphill side. It's the opposite tilt called the self-punishment or "I deserve nothing" attitude. I believe this attitude is less common but is also narcissistic. It refuses grace and takes responsibility to an irresponsible extreme. It refuses help that could prevent harm to themselves and the people who depend on them. Sometimes people get stuck there simply because they want to be disconnected. They don't want to feel obligated to show gratitude or to reciprocate in any way. Teens can get stuck there because of guilt, depression, shame, and even revenge. They don't believe their lives have any value or worth. In this case, these kids need much TLC. They need to feel that they do matter, that their lives do make a difference. In a twisted way kids sometimes use this approach to take revenge and hurt the people who love them. Deep down, though, no kid really wants to be left alone. In all cases, unconditional love rooted in justice and mercy (or steel and velvet) is the model of healthy give-and-take we must work toward in every relationship. Getting a teen's eyes off self is a good first step to reconnect them to a healing balance and a flow of giving and receiving love.

Character Makes a Difference

Character Makes a Difference

Finally, character is power to make a positive difference. It connects and changes the destructive things that happen to us to constructive outcomes through us. I wrote a special poem for Dameon, put it in a frame and presented it to him at the Kamiakin Junior High awards assembly back in 1992. I wanted Dameon to know that no matter what happened to him on the outside, he could use his heart-gifts in hopeful ways. It was titled "Character Standards" and went something like this:

> A man's character is measured by the difference between the—
> Negative he can absorb and the positive he can express.
> Discouragement he faces and the encouragement he gives.
> Suffering he endures and the patience he maintains.
> Pain he feels and the purpose he pursues.
> Criticism he takes and the truth he upholds.
>
> Conflict he tolerates and the peace he intends.
> Setbacks he faces and the persistence he demonstrates.
> Injustice he feels and the mercy he extends.
> Mistakes he makes and the lessons he learns.
> Pressure he faces and the poise he displays.
> Tragedy he endures and triumph he achieves.

Dameon is remembered for the difference his character made. Proverbs 22:1 says, "Choose a good reputation over great riches, for being held in high esteem is better than having silver or gold" (NLT). Dameon was a rich kid.

Chapter Six
Conscience: The Wisdom of an
Inner Brain

Our scientific power has outrun our spiritual power.
We have guided missiles and misguided men.
—Martin Luther King Jr.

The high school football season had ended in disappointment. Our team fell far short of our potential, we lost games that we shouldn't have lost, and team unity seemed nonexistent that year. Even more disappointing, we found out after the season there had been athletic code violations by players on the team. The code was a contract where athletes agreed to abstain from all drug, alcohol, and tobacco use for the privilege of playing sports. I remember my frustration in the spring team meeting and voiced my utter disgust. I had poured my heart into coaching my players, but my young family came first. If I was going to sacrifice my time, it would be for them, not for a bunch of undedicated jocks who didn't care about their team. Coaching wasn't worth the money to me either—especially after figuring out that I made about thirty-five cents an hour. Something needed to change. We needed commitment. Then the players began sharing their own disappointments about their dedication level. The team discussed what they felt they needed to do. Their solution was surprising to me and nearly unanimous. The players wanted drug testing.

On their own, the team captains presented their plan at a school board meeting. But they were shocked when the board determined (with the help of a local lawyer) that drug testing was "against their student rights." But these kids wouldn't be denied. They had experienced the cost of a whole season going down the drain and were ready to set high goals and dedicate themselves to achieve them. Their first step was to get the local Kiwanis Club to sponsor the testing after the board rejected their plan.

According to the players' plan, voluntary drug tests began with the new school year and continued throughout the football season. The first week a few of the guys decided to post their clean test results on their hallway lockers. The idea spread and soon the weekly results appeared on nearly every player's locker. They stood together in their commitment to be drug- and alcohol-free as a team. They had nothing to hide, nothing to fear, and nothing to lose. On Friday and Saturday nights, instead of going to the parties, the players would hang out together. I heard through the grapevine that the party scene pretty much died that year. But the school spirit, team unity, and thirst for pure fun were more alive than I had ever seen before! We had a phenomenal season and made it all the way to the state quarterfinals.

The drug-testing plan was definitely not a witch-hunt for athletic code violators by coaches. Those kinds of strategies are often disastrous to team spirit. But the players driving the idea themselves created a kind of positive peer pressure. Some told me it gave them a good reason to "just say no." And even though it seemed absurd that the school board wouldn't support team drug testing, I believe they did the players a big favor by denying them. Their denial compelled the players to act on their own good conscience voluntarily. They were empowered to make a stand by sheer act of will and unity. Conscience is always behind a good stand, readying the self to sacrifice for the cause. Good conscience also stands behind our nation's constitutional law—compelling and empowering individuals to freely do right things according to God's laws, whether or not man's laws comply.

Conscience is moral intelligence. Moral intelligence can't be measured by GPAs, SATs, or how high an IQ we have. The essence of moral intelligence is wisdom—or how well we use our knowledge for good purposes. Only God is perfectly good. And goodness means being god-like or godly—using personal power with benevolence in mind. To become good, we must develop our moral intelligence.

We've nourished kids' brains, but we've starved their consciences—their "inner brains" that can learn how best to love and be loved. Without an enlightened conscience, teens have no moral compass or inner guidance system to know right from wrong. The quickened teen conscience detects the destructive weapons that cause harm and violence—envy, jealousy, bitterness, resentment, and revenge—all the things that arm kids for war in their survival-of-the-fittest world.

The Origin of Good Conscience

The Origin of Good Conscience

Too many young people today have become unconscious of their conscience. They don't know of this wonderful nature that makes them fully human because they have accepted and even embraced a lie. They believe they must get somewhere else or do something significant in the eyes of their peers in order to be worthwhile, to have value and importance.

The Theory of Evolution of Species is the underlying assumption, or story line, that is playing out this lie in extremely unhealthy ways. The Theory of Evolution hides the glorious fact that teens have a wonderful role in creation despite their worldly position. Their "place" in humanity, in the royal bloodline of divine imagery, can only be discovered under God and through his ordained, created order. Teens are truly players in a dramatic love story that unfolds in the biblical record of history. Teens need a heritage story that does more than link them to an endless regressive food chain.

For that reason, the Creation Story should become a mandated history course in public schools. It doesn't make sense as a science course. Science is only relevant for repeatable things in the laboratory. Evolution belongs there. And the longer it stays there under true science, the more of a myth it will become. As players in the evolution story, teens are minimized to meaningless, loveless words in an amoral science textbook.

History, however, is weighed by the preponderance of evidence and testimony. Creation is history, and the birthplace of reason and science. Teens truly do have a noble place in creation, and a deep soul-memory of it. They have souls and creative abilities with meaningful opportunities to express them in regular, simple, and fresh ways each day. The Creation Story helps them understand this.

The Creation Story teaches about love. God did not create people because He needed anything from us, but to express his goodness to us and through us. Love is the essence of God's sharing nature and is the way that teens were meant to live. Every teen matters. Every teen makes a difference. Every kid has a place in the grand scheme of love. Love requires community. It is a place where we take turns giving and receiving, needing and overflowing, wanting and having. The human soul is a place of communion with God—a sanctuary—where we can learn to love others more freely, fully, and excellently by learning to love and draw near to him.

Young people have been made to discover the qualities of life that run much deeper and richer than the apparent goods of physical or sensual desire. They've been equipped to behold realities beyond the immediacies of felt impulses. They can learn to recognize and appreciate goodness beneath the exterior lack of beauty, brawn, brains, or bank accounts they see in themselves or their peers. Teens are not animals. As members of the human race they've been created with the highest capacity of all—conscience.

This gift of God gives them at least five special inner capacities to sense, know, and respond to spiritual realities in their world. Teens have an inner capacity to see, to have insight and foresight, the capacity to see beyond life's surface level Four Bs to the real substance and significance of things. They have an inner capacity to hear, to contemplate, and understand the real resonating voice of truth in their soul. Taste allows them to discern and develop excellence in skills, style, and social graces. Touch makes them sensitive to understand the pain and needs of others with compassion. Their inner sense of smell helps them to sniff out and avoid foulness and rottenness and appreciate the pleasant spiritual aroma of goodness and beauty. But these capacities must go to school to be developed and exercised.

Wisdom: The Private School inside Us

Wisdom: The Private School inside Us

If we hope to help our teens navigate safely through the minefields of youth culture, they must be trained in wisdom. In 44 B.C. Cicero wrote, "The function of wisdom is discriminating between good and evil." There is a private school inside every teen called The School of Wisdom. It is where every young person can learn about the "goodness of real goodness and the badness of badness." They graduate by distinguishing right from wrong.

Hornet's comment at the end of Zimmy's internet opinion poll suggested wisdom as an alternative to the Four Bs for guidance in life. She pointed to a place beyond the surface level that stopped the teen chat short. Wisdom directs kids to explore the path of the Four Cs. Wisdom directs them to think about what they think, to question how life works best, and to discern good authority and the voice of truth.

The schooling is not easy, but the rewards are great. Scriptures tell us,

Happy is the person who finds wisdom and gains understanding. For the profit of wisdom is better than silver, and her wages are better than gold. Wisdom is more precious than rubies; *nothing you desire can compare with her.* She offers you life in her right hand,

and riches and honor in her left. She will guide you down delightful paths; all her ways are satisfying. Wisdom is a tree of life to those who embrace her; happy are those who hold her tightly (Prov. 3:13–18, NLT, emphasis added).

Amazing! *Nothing* a teen *could desire*—no Four B attraction of sex, money, power, pleasure, or popularity—can compare to the satisfaction of wisdom. God positioned wisdom as the teacher of good conscience. Wisdom speaks:

The LORD formed me from the beginning, before he created anything else. I was appointed in ages past, at the very first, before the earth began. ... I was there when he established the heavens, when he drew the horizon on the ocean. ... I was the architect at his side. I was his constant delight, rejoicing always in his presence. And how happy I was with what he created—his wide world and all the human family!

And so, my children, listen to me, for happy are all who follow my ways. Listen to my counsel and be wise (Prov. 8:22–33, NLT).

Conscience must continually stay enrolled in this school to become a better judge and governor over the self or soul. Good judgments need time and space for deliberation and careful thought. Under the guidance of wisdom the student learns unchangeable laws or truths that operate in the soul realm of relationships just like the laws of gravity operate in the physical realm.

Truth is "with-it"—always relevant and up-to-date on the current state of affairs. Truth is genuine, pure, and real—not fake, diluted, deceitful, or counterfeit. Truth is faithful and steady in responding to every situation or predicament. Truth fosters and protects love and lasting friendships. It keeps promises and maintains good authority. Truth is always in conformity with fact or reality. It is predictable. It is honest, not fraudulent or pretended. It is fair, precise, and consistent with everything that makes people ultimately happiest, healthiest, and most free.

Truth always settles disagreements and arguments the best way, based on debating objective facts and not subjective feelings. It puts everything in proper perspective, order, and place. When truth wins out, it creates unity, harmony, agreement, and peace. Whenever there is not harmony, unity or peace, it means there is an issue. An issue is a problem, conflict or point to be debated. It only means that there may be an error or inconsistency in the assumptions or reasoning in one of the parties involved.

Truth and Taste

James was an angry skateboarding teen who grew up in a home where his parents didn't "force" God on him. They never attended church as a family except for weddings or funerals and believed kids should make up their own minds about religion. James grew up calling his mom and dad by their first names. As a ten year old, he began smoking pot and drinking at home with the approval of his parents. When he was a child, his first dad would slap him around and intimidate him to keep him in line. But problems grew in junior high when James' parents divorced. He didn't feel any adult had the right to tell him what to do—especially when he knew they couldn't hit him. He was suspended from school several times for breaking rules, fighting, and verbally attacking his teachers. He feared none of them and resented most of them. He'd fill his time by hanging out at the skate park by day and partying with friends at night. By high school he couldn't handle the "authoritarian" approach of teachers and administrators so he dropped out. And even though his parents trained him to be a "free thinker," his new stepdad couldn't handle his obnoxious attitude around home and eventually kicked him out.

That's when James got involved with a local youth anarchist group through his skater friends. He finally found a cause that validated his anger and rebellion against all authority. His inner pain was eased by an irrational assumption that there is no "good" authority. He believed that the only goodness was uninhibited expression of his passion. But in his new group, passion found plenty things to hate but little to love or look forward to. The group was very disorganized because members resented leadership, structure, and order. They studied websites on how to be insurrectional and even how to make bombs. The only rallying factor was mutual agreement to destroy the present social structures of authority, with no solid grounds for a good society beyond it.

The painfully empty souls of teens are now being led along this path by educated new morality "experts" (they wouldn't call themselves authorities!). Anarchist publishers, bookstores, and websites are building a profitable social order on the mythical ideas of utopia on the other side of destruction. The philosophy preys upon kids who are alienated, hurting, and angry. They offer confusing ideas that excuse violence but lack the power of love, the strategy of non-violence, and the simplicity of truth.

Eventually James landed a job were he grew to admire and respect his boss, who happened to be a Christian. A relationship developed that revealed the underlying lie of anarchy that there is "no good authority." In James' experience, his boss was an example of loving leadership—a person who was sacrificially fair, honest, and who had his workers' best interests in mind. And the crew worked far better as a team and were much more productive than he had experienced with his former group.

The classroom of wisdom is the real world, not hollow or vain philosophy. Conscience must learn to discern the voice and style of another teacher as well. This teacher is named taste. Taste teaches the selective classes—the ones we do for fun and personal enrichment. Taste knows our preferences very well. In fact, if we attended this school just for our enjoyment, we'd be taking all of our classes from taste. Taste offers us many options of subjects such as personal styles, social life, culture, manners, drama, clothing, careers, foods, sports, games and activities, and the ways of home and family. These courses are easy to take and much more popular.

A friend of mine once told me, "You can't do everything you can do." And this is a truth about taste. The idea never changes. The point of this simple slogan reminds us that life is full of choices. The things we can do are not necessarily things we should do or that lead us to pleasant consequences. With taste in charge, like it was at first in James' life, there are no firm grounds to trust the goodness of authority or delay gratification. Popular vote or violent power replaces natural law, and fifty-one fickle feelings can undermine the destiny of forty-nine true and good convictions.

Taste's highest end is freedom. Truth's highest end is love. When teens submit their wants to what is right, good, and true they will grow in their capacity to love and be loved. However, when teens are told there is no truth, they will only learn to hate everything that resists their freedom of getting what they want. True freedom is not anarchy or the absence of moral fences that restrict expression of our passions on a horizontal, worldly level. Rather, it is the unbound expression of our heart-gifts on a vertical level—to creatively and freely love and be loved within clear moral boundaries for appropriate behavior and care of one another. Freedom is not the absence of authority; it is the good and perfect alignment under God and his good order. And believe it or not, these ideas create freedom in the hearts and minds of kids more than restrict them. Under God, they have the deepest and most complete spiritual freedom. With God as their ultimate protector, they will fear him and have nothing else to fear. With God as their provider, they will trust him and have nothing else to lose.

The Only Two Things Teens Must Do

I attended a workshop on crisis intervention when I was a school administrator. The instructor was a specialist who trained police how to disarm potentially volatile and violent situations. The real take-away value for me could be stated in one sentence, "Good authority always wins out eventually, but you just don't have to win right now." A leader's confidence actually relieves pressure and anger from his or her approach and helps to disarm the situation.

I've appreciated the book, *Parenting Teens with Love and Logic* by Foster Cline, M.D. and Jim Fay. Their words echo the expert advice above when they wrote, "Any time we tell teens to do something we can't make them do, we give them too much control."

There are many things that teens can do and many things that teens should do. But there are only two things that they must do. What parent or teacher has not heard this question from their kids: "Do I have to?" So in order to save some explanation time, one of the basic lessons I taught students was called "The Only Two Things You Must Do in Life."

As you can guess, a variety of goofy adolescent answers followed my initial question of what these two things might be. For instance, "To die and pay taxes" has always been a favorite. But this lesson helped my students form a foundation of motivation beneath everything I taught them. And when this small and simple truth unfolded, a typical hush would come over the room. It is "deep calling to deep" that brings a quieting, reverential peace that resonates in young souls.

So just what were the only two things my students "must do" in life (and in my classroom)? Here's what I taught them:

You have to make choices in life.

You have to live with consequences of the choices you make.

The principle is "sowing and reaping." Choices reap consequences. Some have called it the "Law of the Harvest." We sow the seeds of choice and we reap the harvest of consequences. We can choose our choices, but not our consequences. The timing, intensity, and degree may all vary, but good choices will always reap profits and bad choices will always reap loss—either in what we get or in who we become. The final profit/loss balance statement of our good and bad choices may not be fully realized this side of heaven, but we can count on the accuracy and integrity of the bookkeeper above. Every choice we make, good or bad, will be accounted for in the end. All of our choices bear fruit in two realms—the realm of becoming and the realm of getting. Every decision that we make eventually or immediately affects other people as well. Every kid makes a difference and one single choice can change many lives for better or worse.

The School of Wisdom teaches teens that they have choices—and every choice has consequences. Learning is a choice. The consequences of not fully attending the School of Wisdom are severe. Willpower is the tool teens need to toil well, to work the soil of their hearts to receive truth, and then to act upon it.

Willpower: The Hidden Key to Teachability

"Blessed are those who have a tender conscience, but the stubborn are headed for serious trouble" (Prov. 28:14, NLT). Stubbornness is willpower turned wrong-side out. Stubbornness is a strong will that resists authority. It makes kids hardened and outwardly tough but unreceptive to internal truth. While they are hard on the outside, stubborn people are soft on themselves; they are tender and easy toward their own feelings and whims. The world seems to be very hard on them (in their own opinion).

In contrast, good willpower turns tenderness right-side out. It causes kids to become inwardly tough and willing to pay the price of growth. They become tender and conscientious toward receiving truth. But in a strange turn of events, their outer world becomes much softer on them for some reason. *A tender conscience is a teachable conscience.* Being teachable is a power of the soul that must be exercised with self-discipline—and exercise is often not fun. Correction often feels like an outright offense, no matter who we are. It stings and burns our sense of ego, pride, and self-esteem. It sends an impulse that immediately raises our "stubbornness shield" to protect ourselves. We stop listening. We begin formulating brick walls of blame, excuses, and reasons that our so-called instructor (boss, spouse, neighbor, parent) is wrong.

The state of being teachable is similar to climbing over a mountain.

There is a form of easiness on both ends of the mountain. Camping on the near side is passive. It is lazy and takes no mental effort. It's watching television, playing video games, and goofing off. Making the climb over the mountain is tough, requiring active attention and mental work. But the beauty and wonder found on the downhill side is delightful. The place of delighted attention is the place where the journey of learning becomes engaging and effortless, interesting and fun. It is the absorption of reading a good book or the doing of good work.

> # Wisdom is oftimes nearer when we stoop, than when we soar.
>
> # William Wordsworth, 1725

Walking Humbly with God

Walking Humbly with God

In the 1920s, post-World War I Germany underwent a severe depression. Inflation was so rampant that a person could carry a basket full of paper cash to the store only to have a thief dump the money on the sidewalk and steal the basket. I remember a story about a young girl who lived in Germany during that era. She lived alone with her impoverished mother who sent her to the bakery for bread each morning. The benevolent baker would hand out leftover loaves from the previous day to the poor children in his community.

Since the little girl was very small and weak, the other kids would push their way in front of her, crowding to get the biggest loaves first. Week after week the other kids would fight between themselves for more bread while the little girl would contently stand last in line to receive the smallest loaf. But she would be the only one to look the kind baker in the eye and gratefully say with a smile, "Thank you, Mr. Baker!"

Then one day the little girl came home with the smallest loaf as usual, but it felt unusually weighty. When her mother sliced into the bread she struck something hard. She broke the bread open to discover two gold coins in the middle—months' worth of wages and groceries! Fearing that the baker had accidentally dropped the coins while kneading the dough, the mother sent the girl directly back to return them to him. The little girl arrived promptly and said to the baker, "Sir, you must be missing these gold coins. We found them in our loaf of bread!" But the kind baker smiled at her and said, "No, I put them there just for you!"

God, too, is full of good and kind surprises for the humble and grateful. God has hidden his gold coins, however, in the hearts of those who are in authority over us. Parents have gold coins and rich treasures hidden in their hearts for teachable, obedient kids. We are God's TAs—teacher assistants. "Children, obey your parents in the LORD, for this right. 'Honor your father and your mother' (this is the first commandment with a promise), 'that it may be well with you and that you may live long on the earth' " (Eph. 6:1–3, RSV).

The first order of bless-ability for teens is to maintain a teachable spirit toward their parents. The habit of humility before our earthly parents foreshadows a humble walk with our heavenly Father. To have such an eternal influence on our kids is an enormous responsibility for parents. It should bring us to our knees!

The modeling opportunities parents possess are irreplaceable. Parents, more than anyone, can impress young hearts and minds with the pattern and purpose of godly power—servant leadership. One of the most lasting memories I have of my dad is seeing him leaning over the kitchen sink, doing the dinner dishes. Besides being the sole income earner in our home, after a long day's work Dad still served our family this way nearly every night. Using authority properly is a powerful, but indirect lesson. It's an irony that preaches a million wordless sermons to teens.

The world certainly provides plenty of contrasts to servant leadership to our kids. My heart sank just the other day when we parked next to a pickup truck at Papa Murphy's Pizza. The man in the driver's seat—either the father or the boyfriend, I couldn't tell for sure—unleashed a string of threatening and profane words at the kids in the backseat. It was clear that he had little care for the wounds he made on their hearts. The sexual innuendoes on his window decals seemed to reveal his attitude about the lady he sent inside as well. Power is typically lorded over teens by self-indulgent adults. Loving leadership that is both strong and sympathetic aligns with God's power and purpose.

The first task of the parent/teacher is to know one's subject well. But the primary subject matter for the best, most effective teachers is not the lesson but the learner. Research proves that the student-teacher relationship is the most critical factor in learning. Teachers must certainly have good knowledge of the information, the illustrations, and the applications of the lesson at hand.

The expert teacher is like a gardener. He has learned how to garden the hearts, heads, and hands of the student. The greatest rewards for the good teacher are reaped well after the paychecks stop coming. The reward is revisiting the patch of soil that years before was hardened and parched. It is recalling the laborious tilling, sowing, and watering of good seeds of truth. Finally, it is realizing the once barren ground has become a fruitful garden, one that is producing its own seeds for posterity. An expert teacher brings kids to an awareness of what God has already planted in their souls, to expand and refine those gifts to reap benefits for a community.

A second task of the parent/teacher is to turn life experiences into object lessons. This helps kids recognize the transparency of the surface world. To help them see through tangible things to the patterns and beauty behind them. Peter Kreeft is one of my favorite contemporary authors. He is a philosophy professor at Boston College, well-informed and passionate about the teachings of C.S. Lewis. In his book, *C.S. Lewis for the Third Millenium*, Kreeft writes:

> True joy is significance; false joy is power. True joy is finding truth and choosing goodness and beauty. False joy is fabricating ideologies and "creating your own values" and buying beauty. True joy is smelling a rose; false joy is plucking and possessing it. … Everything is not only a thing, but a sign, full of significance. Modernity, confining itself to the scientific method as the model for knowing reality, deliberately induces in itself what Lewis calls a dog-like state of mind, full of facts and empty of significance. Point to your dog's food and he will sniff your finger.

Wisdom sends us back to our childhood.

Pascal

The Significance of the Teen Self

The Significance of the Teen Self

One morning I told my teen Sunday school class that we were going to do an experiment. I'd asked a preschool teacher if she'd help by bringing in some of her kids—I had some money for them. One at a time, I had each preschooler come up to the front of my class where I offered each child a choice. I held out a nickel in one hand and a dime in the other. The child could choose the coin he or she thought was the best.

Without exception, each young child picked the nickel. It was actually pretty funny—and we cheered for them. The choice seemed obvious—bigger definitely meant more. The nickels were definitely the best choice.

But the children taught us all something about ourselves that day. After our little nickel experiment I asked my students what they observed and why they thought the children all picked the nickel instead of the dime. My students, then, were called upon to teach me what they learned in the lesson. A few began raising their hands and offering ideas.

"Sometimes what we think is most important isn't really important at all!"

"Bigger doesn't always mean better!" another chimed in.

"And why is that so?" I asked.

"Because sometimes people just don't understand—we only look on the outside of things. We don't know what things are really worth."

"And what are our nickel choices?" I asked. The question silently sank into deeper levels of their adolescent hearts.

Just what did the preschoolers teach us? Isn't it that we're all preschoolers at heart? Proudly and confidently, we judge by outward appearance. We make choices based on childish ideas of what works and how we get the most out of life. Faster is better, bigger is better—I quantify before I qualify.

Until teens understand the real significance stamped on their souls—that they belong to God, that he made them and paid for them, that he has assigned eternal value to them—they will keep choosing things that appear bigger in the world's eyes. Because God has imprinted his image on their hearts, it doesn't matter how the world measures them.

Outcome Based Education is the current trend in education. It emphasizes performance in standardized tests. It majors on measuring scores and mastering certain content above love of learning. It's an outer curriculum, pragmatic view that leads kids to believe that the *summon bonum* of schooling is to manipulate their world somehow to their advantage. Pragmatism leads us to use people and love things.

> # Men have become tools of their tools.
> ### —Thoreau, Walden Pond

Over 1,500 years ago Saint Augustine illustrated a potential dilemma that adopting a purely pragmatic view of life creates. He simply compared a pearl to a mouse. He first asked which would we prefer to have, a pearl or a mouse. A pearl, obviously! A pearl is a much more valuable possession. But which of the two would we prefer to be? Certainly, a mouse! A living creature has potential to grow toward *perfection*. It has power to act that a lifeless stone does not—no matter how attractively coated it might be! Mortimer Adler also observed the reason for preferring to be a mouse rather than a pearl is also the reason for preferring to be a good rather than a bad person. Our souls have developmental capacities for growth in doing greater good. In real capacity, even the smallest sparrow in the world is more valuable than the biggest pearl.

It is a true art to see beneath the immediate and apparent things of life to the hidden curriculum, the real meaning and value of things. Our system for determining the worth of people is often the one we use for things. When souls are in the mix, sometimes less is more. I saw this wonderfully illustrated another way, relating to the unborn child. A baby in the womb is not an inert mass of tissue. He or she holds inside the wonder of human growth and worth!

A woman stood up front at church one Sunday morning and shared a short message. She took a dollar bill out of her pocket and asked a gentleman in the front row to come forward. She asked him if he wanted the dollar bill. Of course, he did. But before she handed it to him, the woman crushed the dollar in her hand, threw it down on the ground and mashed it into the floor under her foot. Then she asked, "Do you still want it?" Of course he did. The gentleman stooped down, picked up the deformed dollar bill off the carpet, unfolded it, placed it in his pocket, and sat down. No matter what it looked like on the outside, the dollar didn't lose its real value. This illustration was presented on Pro-Life Sunday.

I've seen many "crumpled-up" kids and adults who, in their brokenness, have made an immense impact for good. It is the disfigured girl who shows kindness, the one-legged boy who hopped as a running back for the high school football team, the seventh-grade girl with cerebral palsy who stocks books at the school library on Saturday as her service project, the eighty-year-old man who washes dishes for a living and sends in a dollar to help a sick child. Nothing changes our felt quality of life faster than these kinds of clarifying contrasts. It is the sudden realization that beauty can be veiled by brokenness. Those who exercise good character despite adversity, who leverage their heart-gifts against personal hardships, these are perhaps the most powerful, disarming presences in schools today.

I grew up as a late-blooming, fourth-born kid in a sports-oriented family of five brothers. From hands and knees football in our home hallway, to a cardboard box basketball hoop hanging on a kitchen cupboard—I was weaned on competition. Perhaps the deepest, most valuable lesson I learned was that Mom and Dad loved us no matter how we performed on the field or at home. Yes, we were painfully disciplined at times, but it was meant for our best. Our basic sense of worth and acceptance was not based on performance. We mattered because of who we were, not just because of what we did. My growing up experience was a powerful unspoken lesson that only recently have I been able to articulate. My parents released a truth in me at the soul level. I learned that

> # failure is just a learning experience when rejection isn't a factor.

Sometimes we buy into the performance-oriented, pragmatic view of self-worth. If we fail to meet certain standards, realistic or not, we feel unworthy of love. This wrongly blocks the flow of truth and love to us and through us. But real guilt and actual offenses toward God and others are different. They really do alienate us from relationship. A guilty conscience is a healthy warning signal that our actions may have damaged a connection. To restore relationship we must confess and ask forgiveness for the way we may have wounded others. A healthy conscience acts like spiritual radar to warn us or detect any potential damage that our deeds have done. The goal of a clean conscience is not simply to free us from feelings of guilt, but to restore right relationship with God and others.

Teens are wired internally to matter, to be loved. When they sense they are valued unconditionally, it leads them to trust. When they sense their value is conditioned on their performance or appearance it breeds fear of failure and rejection. Love is a sanctuary of non-rejection. Love creates a culture that embraces young people where they are and releases them to become the best they were meant to be. When they are rooted in healthy relationships, the best measurable results blossom from their lives. But a successful life on the soul level is all about having healthy relationships, not merely getting measurable results.

It is God's truth that guides teens through their cultural minefield. It is the flow of God's love in and through them that disarms their hearts. The inner curriculum of the Four Cs is a challenging course. It's a mountain. It is not for those young people who are totally satisfied with their lives, for those who've "arrived." This course is for those who may have money but still feel poor inside. It is for those who want to be accepted but rarely feel acceptable. It is for those who look at school and grades and the success it's supposed to give us and ask, "Why?" It's for those who want to care about others but can't seem to get past their own hurts.

Conscience keeps us connected in relationship to truth and love at the place of our deepest heart need. And it maintains that connection by seeing it through to our highest purpose. It connects upwardly from the taproot of faith through character formation to courage-building and then through the exercise of compassion. And compassion's end is not only *to serve people,* but ultimately through people to serve and please the heart of the author of compassion—to glorify him.

The consciences of teens learn to recognize and respond like James did to loving leadership, to unite them like a team in causes to do what's right, and to humbly receive the gifts of benevolent authority like the grateful girl who discovered gold coins in her bread. And no matter how they appear on the outside, their consciences help them embrace the embrace of God.

The wise want love; and those who love want wisdom.

—Shelley

Chapter Seven
Teaching Kids to Do Heroic Things

Chapter Seven
Teaching Kids to Do Heroic Things

Action is eloquence.
—Shakespeare

When my daughter Jaclyn was about five years old, I taught her the "trust fall." I stood her up on the edge of the couch and faced her away from me. Then I stood behind her with my arms ready and explained the game.

"Jaclyn," I said, "You can't see me, but you know who this is talking to you, don't you?"

Knowing well her father's voice she said, "Yes, it's you, Daddy!"

"Honey," I said, "if you fell backwards, do you think your daddy is strong enough to catch you?"

"Yeah," she replied, with a note of excited curiosity.

"And Jaclyn, do you think Daddy loves you so much that I would never let you fall?"

"Yes!" Her answer was immediate.

"Then I'm going to ask you to do something scary—I want you to trust me. When I count to three, I want you to fall backwards into my arms without looking. Okay?"

"Okay," she said, hesitating briefly.

So I counted, "Ready, one, two, three!"

Then with a slight peek over her shoulder and quivering knees, she sat back in my arms. "Great, Jaclyn!" I applauded her courage.

But then, to my surprise, the moment I put her feet on the floor she hopped back up on the couch with confidence and said, "Daddy, that was fun. Let's do it again!" And this time, without delay she blindly fell back stiff as a board! Simple as a child's fall, this was a picture of faith to me.

Hard to say, but I think this little game did please me more than Jaclyn. What brought me most joy as a father? My child found comfort in my arms and confidence in me. Her faith in action took her from "head knowledge" of her daddy's power and goodness to "heart knowledge" of it—and then she proved it by taking her next joy-filled risk of falling again.

I believe this little activity helped to anchor a deep truth in Jaclyn's heart for the stormy teenage passage we later faced together. After Michael's ordeal, we navigated through some very turbulent and heart-breaking years with her. But nothing could replace the sense of God's unfailing grip of love on her heart as a child. Now, as a young woman, she is returning to that safe place of faith in God's care. She is again discovering the arms of a Father who loves her too much and is too strong to ever let her fall. Tenderly, he leads us all back to such places of trust.

> # "The eternal God is your refuge, and his everlasting arms are underneath you" (Deuteronomy 33:27, NLT).

Taking the Plunge of Trust

The deepest need and highest purpose in the teen heart is love. Young people long to experience the realness and goodness of loving arms beneath them and lofty, heroic goals before them. But learning to love and be loved cannot happen apart from trust. Blinded except for desire, many teens stand on the edges of uncertainty in life with little hope for help beyond their immediate senses. They grasp for anything that feels real to keep them from falling into despair. I've heard plenty of adults taking potshots at young people today, comparing how disrespectful kids are now to the way they once were. But it's my observation that modern kids have a more difficult time trusting the goodness of authority, obeying parents, and denying the temptations for gratification. For them, it's a frightening plunge of faith.

Adults are responsible for physical and emotional abuse as well as scandals and abandonment. These disappointments make our kids distrust and disrespect the adult world. Peers seem more understanding and less hypocritical; teens see friends as more realistic and responsible than we adults do. So who can blame them for trusting their perceptions?

As a former public school teacher, I've especially felt the need to earn back the trust of teens. I do know they have noses for phonies and sniff them out miles away. For teens to take the plunge and put their faith in adult authority, they need reliable, Shin-like leaders of steel and velvet. Adults who act consistently with their stated values and have kids' best interests in mind offer open arms that convincingly invite teens.

Parents are the most important teachers, and the home is the most important school our kids will ever attend. So it's vital that we continually grow, steely and velvety, to win back the trust of alienated teens. I'm in the process of raising five kids and working with thousands more; I'm the first to admit that I'm not an expert—I just have many experiences to share. I'm still learning and have many emotional bumps and bruises to show for it.

One thing I do know, my children have helped to bring my own character flaws to the surface. I've learned that my first impulses of toughness or tenderness tend to indulge my desires rather than my kids' best interest. When they've misbehaved, I've tended to show my anger and defensiveness more than my hurt and disappointment. I've learned how we parents can look so good in front of our peers, while inner defiance hides behind the outward compliance of our kids. I'm also learning that inner compliance is won in the long-term with love, not fear.

Navigational Aides for Teens

God designed the principle of authority to work like magnetic north. It is an outer power we trust to give us bearing, direction, and leadership in life. God is love, and he has also hardwired his image-bearers with four navigational aides or "bearing finders" of compassion, courage, character, and conscience to help us walk in his ways of mercy, justice, goodness, and truth. We must learn to trust the way God inwardly empowered us to find and walk this path of love.

Parents, mentors, and teachers play a special role as trustworthy guides in this journey. We hope that our teens will grow to become internally guided by God. We pray their hearts will be oriented to his true north and experience direction through their own Four Cs to act justly, love mercy, and to walk humbly with their God. But until they do, our lives leave a natural breadcrumb trail behind us for our direction-hungry kids. The question is, are we leading them on paths of gold or chasing our own Four B rainbows? Time will tell. Our children and their children eventually build highways over the trails we blaze. Our lives leave a legacy of greater or lesser sanctuary in posterity.

Leading by Example

There is an old saying among teachers: "Kids learn in three ways. By example, by example, and by example." Good leaders earn the trust of their followers because of the good places they bring us to. Winning the trust of our teens is hard-earned. But it is also the most rewarding and important part of teaching, coaching, and parenting. Faith in good authority brings hope. And hope motivates us to love sacrificially. And when we love we become leaders who inspire and encourage others to love as well.

I had the privilege of playing college football for four years at the University of Washington under the legendary coach Don James. My fifth year I was also an undergraduate assistant coach while I completed my degree. Coach James is small in physical stature but huge in sheer presence. He had an open-door policy for all his players, but only the brave few dared to enter. I think I have a better idea of what "Fear of the Lord" means after being around this man. He was a great example to me of good authority—his character and countenance commanded respect, but he also genuinely cared and was extremely loyal to his players and fellow coaches.

Those people who were under his guidance knew Coach James represented the epitome of leadership, goal setting, and hard practice. His solid football program was built on the foundation of his work ethic, organization, and his attention to detail in following through. But he also modeled excellence and integrity in his own life—he "walked his talk" and truly cared about his players. And he wouldn't allow profanity on the football field either. One time another coach told me he was especially tired and weary of the long hours he had put in a particular week. He grumbled to himself about going home late another night, only to have Coach James pass him in the office hallway carrying his toothbrush and wearing his pajamas. His leadership earned the trust of his coaches and players. And his winning football record was remarkable.

Leading Teens to Experience their Four Cs

The Book of Proverbs is my leadership manual for understanding the behaviors of the Four Cs. There are thirty-one chapters in the book, and it has been my morning exercise for several years to read one chapter every day of every month. Proverbs is all about doing right things. And in teaching the Four Cs to kids, nothing can replace the eloquence of action. The Bible says, "But be doers of the word, and not hearers only ..." (James 1:22, RSV). Just as faith without good works is dead, words without deeds are empty. In the fourth century B.C., Aristotle wrote, "We become just by performing just actions, temperate by performing temperate actions, brave by performing brave actions." Teaching with action happens in two ways— by the examples we are and the experiences we stage for our kids.

Guy Clark sings a country song titled "Stuff That Works." I first heard the refrain in the movie *The Rookie* and it goes like this ...

Stuff that works
Stuff that holds up
The kind of stuff you don't hang on the wall.
Stuff that's real
Stuff you feel
The kind of stuff you reach for when you fall.

(Stuff That Works. Words and Music by Guy Clark and Rodney J. Crowell, © 1994, EMI APRIL MUSIC, INC., GSC MUSIC, and SONY/ATV TUNES, LLC. All rights for GSC MUSIC controlled and administered by EMI APRIL MUSIC, INC. All rights reserved. International copyright secured. Used by permission.)

Kids need real "stuff" to lean on and to learn from. Real life experiences cause kids to call upon and reach out with their Four Cs. When teens fall into doubt and temptation, conscience reaches out to grasp truth to gain real wisdom. When they fall into depression, character reaches out to grasp goodness to gain real hope. When they fall into opposition, courage reaches out to grasp justice to gain real strength. When they fall into self-absorption, compassion reaches out to mercy to gain a sense of real love. God's truth, goodness, justice, and mercy can't be hung on the wall, but they are the real stuff that can hold anyone when they fall. As adult leaders, we are responsible to set the stage for teens to discover this real stuff, both inside them and high above them.

Doing

In 1752 Benjamin Franklin staged an experiment with lightning. He tied a key to the string of a kite and flew it in a thunderstorm. Lightning struck and sent a charge through the kite to the key and he discovered it to be electricity. In 1992, I witnessed a different kind of lightning bolt strike the hearts of teens at Kamiakin Junior High in Kirkland, Washington. Compassion for Michael charged hundreds of young people to do heroic acts of service to save his life. The lightning sparked a cause in the hearts of teens. It lit up their minds with helpful ideas, energized their hands to work hard, and electrified the community as well. It was real stuff, but you can't hang it on a wall either.

In 1995 I began flying a "kite" called Sparrow Clubs, a youth-based charity. The "key" was to connect more kids in medical crisis to schools as inspirational causes for community service. At first, it was an experiment to see if the lightning would strike again in young hearts and spark something powerful in kids. It did—and has many times over. Even though impulses of empathy, like lightning bolts, are rare uncontrollable phenomena, I believe there is hard wiring for the electricity of compassion in the souls of kids.

Compassion is a powerful current of love that does carve a deep path in every young person's heart. We need not wait for accidental storms of life to charge heart-paths with compassion. We found there are plenty of medically broken kids in every community who need help. And there are plenty of passionate, idealistic young people who long to do heroic things. We simply connect young hearts to the real cause of helping a broken child. Both sets of needs are factors in a formula similar to multiplication, the product of two negatives becomes positive in Sparrow Clubs. This is not an ingenious new idea—it's just a reality that we bumped into, perhaps divinely orchestrated for such a time as this, especially with the threat of youth violence on the rise. It is truly the power of one—one small sparrow that flies like a kite and sparks a real experience of love in schools. Courage, character, and conscience are connected to this same circuit of love that God designed.

Treasuring the Treasures inside Teens

Teens

I know the gold is there, but the prospectors are few. Many must be trained to see the signs, to mine, and then refine the buried treasures in young people's hearts. The deep nature of teens hasn't changed, but it takes practice to see the Four Cs through all the artificial layers their world puts upon them. The quality of our recognition of kids' heart-gifts determines the quality of their response to them. To the extent that we recognize and encourage their heart-gifts is the extent of a teen's response. Our recognition also influences the level of our sincerity and enthusiasm to mentor and encourage our teens.

One of our physically broken "sparrows," a baby named AvonLeah, was born premature with severe brain damage that caused blindness and cerebral palsy. AvonLeah was "adopted" by the local high school as their "sparrow" and the kids did heartwarming service projects on her behalf. We do point to the significance of teen's actions by what we reward with recognition. AvonLeah's dad, Matt Jacobson, pointed to the real significance of what the teens did in a beautifully written letter to the *Nugget* newspaper editor. He publicly recognized and rewarded their actions when he wrote the following:

> There is a standard, given long ago, for the governance of everyone's actions in the community—"Do unto others as you would have them do unto you." Lisa and I would like to extend our deepest gratitude to the students of Sisters High School who, through The Sparrow Club's first event, made a tremendously profound statement to us and to the community.
>
> You reached beyond the confines and comfort of your own world into the life of a little one too weak to be her own advocate. It was a divine act, really, filled with the unmistakable power that always accompanies truth, well spoken. By your actions, you declared to a world adrift on the ocean of competing values: It matters not if you aren't "perfect," your life still has meaning, It matters not if you are weak, your life still has purpose. It matters not if you are small, you still have value. We hope that you are able to see the gift that you've given and that the seed of this gift will grow into a mighty oak under which we all embrace the value of a life, wherever we find it.

Matt recognized the real stuff of the sparrow project. The gift of the kids went far beyond the money raised for his little girl. Their heroic love put a higher dimension of value and meaning to AvonLeah's struggle. He saw the treasures inside teens and responded with sincere appreciation—something teens are starved for today.

Training Eyes to See Another's Needs

Training Eyes to See Another's Needs

Besides being trained to recognize and treasure the treasures inside kids, I believe we can be trained to see the real needs in one another as well. To me, Marianne always looks the same. Her eyes gazing in a distant stare, her mouth partially open, hands clasped closed across her lap. She was born very healthy, but when she was a baby her father shook her in anger. She is now eight years old and bound to a wheelchair, restricted for life, unable to walk or talk. Dad got locked away in a different kind of prison, but likely not for life like his innocent little girl is. Mom is strong. She is sensitive. She struggles to survive and care for Marianne and her sister on her own. It's amazing how she can read every invisible emotion on her little girl's face—from fright to delight. It is a mystery to me how this mother's eyes and mine can behold the same face of a child, yet how much more her soul has learned to see.

Marianne was adopted by a middle school. The students earned Sparrow Cash—seed money sponsored by a local business—by stacking firewood for elderly people, shoveling snow, and doing a talent show. Marianne attended the school assembly the kids arranged as a celebration for her. Afterward, when students were crowding around Marianne, a boy came up to me with seventeen dollars his grandpa gave him for Christmas presents. He wanted to know how he should give it to his sparrow. Like Marianne's mom, he learned to see a greater need than his own and responded by doing something. Seeing needs is more a matter of having an open heart, I think, than just having open eyes. Even though it was hard to receive a boy's Christmas money, I was thrilled to help him begin the giving journey.

The Real Heartbeat of Community Service

The Real Heartbeat of Community Service

The educational world is validating the value of kids doing volunteer work. Community service is now being mandated in many schools. It is a good thing, but I've found that the delivery method is really the key to the take-away value for kids. When community service is perceived as a pressure thing, service loses its true significance. Kids must own the cause. Requiring service for graduation can make volunteering seem like just another hoop for teens to jump through to get something or somewhere else—not as a higher end or to point to something significant flowing deep in the soul like true love.

I do believe, however, that mandated service can be "redeemed" by adding the elements of the Four Cs. Compassion adds a heartbeat to community service. Impulses of empathy and the electricity of compassion resuscitate the hearts of teens. Even in required projects, students who are deeply touched by mercy, who have their own pain drained in the brokenness of another, these kids forget about the credits and go above and beyond the call of duty. And I believe the key to compassion is hidden in the power of a powerless one.

> ## One cannot weep for the entire world. It is beyond human strength. One must choose.
> ### —Jean Anouilh

Truth and love resonate in teens' hearts when impulses of empathy and kindness touch them. These impulses cannot be controlled, but they can be fostered through the educational stages we establish. So often we allow these heartbeats of real love to fade away like retreating footsteps. But these very impulses, I believe, symbolize something deeply meaningful to the way God wired kids for happiness. And the impulses are truly ironic and contrary to the notion of evolution, where mercy has no logical place in its survival-of-the-fittest scheme. The Theory of Evolution blinds the soul the way cataracts blind the eyes—it has no room for peripheral vision or a higher view of life.

Happiness is determined by the flow of God's love in and through us. It's influenced by what we say and do. Conscience and character enlarge our inner borders for a greater flow of love. Courage and compassion make connections and empower that love-flow. Courage overcomes resistance to love—whether that resistance is outer injustices or inner fears. And compassion connects us to the real needs of others and releases that love in healing and helpful ways.

Teens can hear the voice of conscience and they must choose to follow it. The real goal is to help teens intentionally use their heart-gifts of courage and compassion to love and be loved.

Courage Called Out by Challenges
Courage Called Out by Challenges nges

Compassion may be called out by a subtle whisper of another's pain. But courage is "dared-out" by bold challenges. Young people need to be dared to do healthy but difficult things. I remember a time when the San Francisco '49ers had just picked my teammate and friend Mike Baldassin to try out for their team. I recall bumping into Coach James and enthusiastically asking what he thought about Mike's chances. Coach knew his players well and he didn't waste words. He precisely said, "Don't tell Mike Baldassin that he *can* make it. Tell him he *can't*." That was that. I thanked Coach and walked away having to figure out what he meant.

Mike played linebacker and didn't have the physical gifts of size and speed to be a top prospect even in coming to the University of Washington. Coach James knew Mike faced long odds of making it in the pros. But Coach was a great strategist and knew his player's competitive strengths. Mike was a passionate player at heart. He became our team captain and set a school record in tackles. His real assets for overcoming adversities were buried deeper than his physical abilities, measurable tools, and talents. I believe the same principle operates in the heart of every teen. It takes good coaches to call that out in them. Mike beat Coach James' dare and played three years of pro football.

Teens long to be brave lovers, to face daring challenges for the sake of rich relationships. Kids are much more likely to take risks than we adults are. They approach pain and rally around their friends who need help much more quickly than we do. They are more open to share their vulnerability as well. Dr. Robert Schuller built a ministry around "Possibility Thinking"—encouraging people to "believe" in order to "achieve." But sometimes it takes "Impossibility Thinking" to dare-out the best in kids, like $175,000 in a few weeks. We must set the stage for their faith to be rooted in God's power rather than their own power. Only massive dreams and impossibility have the faith-power to pull teens out of the everyday fray of school life. Often it's only the most wild and wooly, daring and challenging things that tap into teens' true heart-gifts. To young hearts fashioned by God with eternal capacities to share his love, don't tell them what they can do, but with a twinkle in your eye tell them what they can't do!

Poets are typically not pragmatic. But God is both poetic *and* pragmatic. His love works best to meet our deepest needs and reach our highest purposes. His ways do make a measurable difference! God's truth is a template that forms good desires and trains our impulses. And good impulses liberate teens. It's like electricity under control in their souls. They become genuinely compassionate and spontaneous. They fully and freely enjoy life. They courageously take on heroic causes—all with a clear conscience. They become teachable, bless-able, honorable, and loveable. Sowing seeds of soul perfection eventually reaps good fruits outwardly, too—better grades, solid friendships, physical wellness, improved appearance, and avoidance of drugs, alcohol, sex, and violence. By driving toward the Four Cs teens will get more smiles per hour!

Real love, the kind that builds healthy intimacy and community, can overcompensate for "feel" love. A study published in May 2001 titled "Emerging Answers" reviewed research findings on programs to reduce teen pregnancy. The study looked at a wide range of interventions including media campaigns, increased access to family planning and contraceptives, sex education classes, communication with parents, programs for disadvantaged youth, vocational and early education—and service learning. Here is what the study reports:

Service-learning programs may have the strongest evidence of any intervention that they reduce actual teen pregnancy rates while the youth are participating in the program. … Service-learning programs include two parts (1) voluntary service by teens in the community (e.g. tutoring, working in nursing homes, and fixing up parks and recreation areas), and (2) structured time for preparation and reflection before, during, and after service (e.g., group discussions, journal writing, and papers). Sometimes the service is part of an academic class. … Although the research does not clearly indicate why service-learning is so successful, several possibilities seem plausible: participants develop relationships with program facilitators, they gain a sense of autonomy and feel more competent in their relationships with peers and adults, and they feel empowered by the knowledge that *they can make a difference in the lives of others* [emphasis added].

Evidence suggests that doing heroic things like helping others displaces the desire to use others. Service makes a difference. It's clear that the Four Cs are habits of the heart that facilitate this love connection and flow. But are there specific things that we can do and our teens can do to reinforce the Four Cs? And do those choices make a measurable difference in positive consequences for youth? Yes!

Search Institute: The 40 Developmental Assets

I attended a training seminar to become an Asset Ambassador. The workshop presenter opened the session with some concerning statistics. Out of twenty-five industrial nations, the United States was reported to have the most millionaires and the largest government budget. However, we also have the highest youth suicide, the least protection from gun violence, and lowest birth weight. We spend $110 billion annually on drug prevention yet still have the distinction of most drug overdoses. Academically we ranked near the bottom in math and science scores, twenty-first out of the twenty-five nations. The tide has been turning this way for the last thirty to forty years. Why has community spirit left us and how do we get it back?

The purpose of the Ambassador training was to build our awareness of 40 Developmental Assets (see Appendix 2) as specific ways to fortify our communities to meet teen needs. The 40 Assets are the nuts and bolts of experiences that build the Four Cs. I have also identified at least 28 of the 40 Assets as factors that can be experienced in Sparrow Club service projects. These factors are determined to be critical for young people's character growth. The basis for the 40 Assets came from years of research by Search Institute. The Minnesota-based nonprofit organization surveyed over 250,000 sixth- through twelfth-graders across the United States. The results of the surveys clearly identified specific things teens need to succeed, and that our investment in them will pay off dearly in the end. The 40 Assets change the toxic trends of violence, racism, drug and alcohol abuse, and pre-marital sex in youth culture. Basically, the study shows that healthy kids come from healthy communities.

The 40 Assets are separated into twenty external and twenty internal building blocks of success. The more teens associate these assets with their lives, the more dramatically hopeful their future becomes.

The first twenty assets are external. They are sorted into four categories including: *Support, Empowerment, Boundaries and Expectations,* and

Constructive Use of Time. These are things parents and communities can do to set the stage giving teens experiences that will help them succeed. For example:

Asset #1 is under Support: FAMILY LIFE PROVIDES HIGH LEVELS OF LOVE AND SUPPORT.

Asset #7 is under Empowerment: YOUNG PEOPLE PERCEIVE THAT ADULTS IN THE COMMUNITY VALUE YOUTH.

Search Institute introduces the twenty internal assets this way:

A community's responsibility for its young does not end with the provision of external assets. There needs to be a similar commitment to nurturing the internalized qualities that guide choices and create a sense of centeredness, purpose, and focus. Indeed, shaping internal dispositions that encourage wise, responsible, and compassionate judgments is particularly important in a society that prizes individualism.

The twenty internal assets are categorized under: *Commitment to Learning, Positive Values, Social Competencies,* and *Positive Identity.* These are all choices teens can make. For example:

Asset #21 is under Commitment to Learning: YOUNG PERSON IS MOTI-VATED TO DO WELL IN SCHOOL.

Asset #26 is under Positive Values: YOUNG PERSON PLACES HIGH VALUE ON HELPING OTHERS.

The Search Institute survey shows how the 40 Assets protect teens from high-risk behaviors and how they also promote positive life habits. For instance, low-asset kids who were identified as possessing only zero to ten assets report 53 percent problem alcohol use, 42 percent illicit drug use, 33 percent sexual activity, and 61 percent violent behavior. Compare these low-asset teens' risk behaviors with those possessing thirty-one to forty assets. High-asset youth report only 3 percent alcohol problems, 1 percent illicit drug use, 3 percent sexual activity, and 6 percent likelihood of violence.

On the positive behavior side, 53 percent of high-asset youth report succeeding in school compared to 7 percent in the low-asset category; 83 percent high-asset youth report valuing diversity compared to 34 percent in low-asset; 88 percent high-asset youth report maintaining good health compared to 25 percent in low asset; and 72 percent high-asset youth report delaying gratification compared to 27 percent with low assets.

The Four Cs and the 40 Assets do make a difference. But it is clear that spectacular successes must come from unspectacular disciplines. True communities care about little people and they take care of little details. As adult manager-stewards who are responsible to oversee our communities, we would be wise to apply the assets. If we do, our communities will be sanctuaries for our kids.

Culture Changes by the Stories We Tell

We Tell

In the Renaissance era the masses couldn't read, so the priestly order of the day ordained artists and architects to paint, sculpt, and build messages of spiritual truth into their cathedrals through art and architecture. Truth was communicated in pictures and symbols rather than written words. As the people were rooted in spiritual understanding the period became fruitful in scientific discovery and great artwork. Rich in contemplation, the common person could read the tangible fingers pointing to heavenly things. But the common person also discerned earthly things with downright common sense.

Teens today are illiterate and ignorant in matters of the soul. They are not being taught to read the language of real love or absolute truth. They cannot calculate the long-term costs versus benefits of their choices on the quality of persons they are becoming. They are unable to figure the highest return of happiness as they invest their lives into things. They are becoming faster and cleverer at finding out ways to feel distinct and stand out from the crowd, like tattooing and piercing themselves. But they can't sense the prods that herd them along with the crowd.

To restore understanding of real stuff we can't just craft our Four C messages in art, architecture, the written word, or other surface ways. We must skillfully sculpt the Four Cs message by our loving leadership, by heart-engaging experiences, and by the stories we tell. If we are eloquent in these actions, rather than forcing teens to behave certain ways we will win their hearts to want better things. As teens discover and apply Four Cs, their lives will be governed by faith, hope, and love instead of being driven by feelings, impulses, and self-protecting indulgence.

The stories we tell of our heroes help teens understand the real stuff they are made of too. The stuff is found in Dameon's gift and the sanctuary of adaptive PE. It's the homeless father of a family who found a wallet on a Seattle sidewalk, who returned it to the police station with over one thousand dollars in it. Inspiring stories sculpt young people's dreams and paint vivid pictures of the heroic things they are called to do. I invite you to turn to the next chapter and become acquainted with the Four Cs in story form.

Chapter Eight
Four C Stories for the Literate Soul

Literature is my utopia.
—Helen Keller

People are changed by stories. Stories indirectly communicate moral messages. Every human, by nature, deeply resents being told what we should or shouldn't do. That is why people need divine grace to hear from God in true humility and to accept what is best for us. Perhaps that is why Jesus delivered truth couched mostly in acts of kindness and stories of goodness. Perhaps his teaching methods were themselves acts of grace to deliver the soul-saving medicine of submission to God in a form people could palate. It seems, too, his message was most direct only to those who knew his love most intimately and trusted him fully. Or, it was pointedly direct to those who needed to fear him before they would ever hear him.

The Four Cs must be understood in action and put into action. It takes action to change our affections and to build a lasting legacy—a good story—with our lives. Stories have characters who share something in common with us—it purely boils down to human nature. We empathically experience the drama of human dilemma. We observe the ways people choose to respond in belief and behavior. And from a safe distance, our souls can feast on the fruits of consequences born from those beliefs and behaviors—good and bad. Moral lessons help us to be godly.

The indirectness of story morals means we must be wary of the media messages our kids are tuning in to. Every story attunes a deep chord of goodness and badness or rightness and wrongness that resonates in our kids' souls. The characters, choices, and consequences in story speak for themselves. The message subtly articulates how to be a hero or a lover. For that is the unspoken dream of every teen. The question is, do the chain of events in the message ring true to real life? The consequences of story subtly shape beliefs that eventually play out through behaviors in significant ways.

The Book of Virtues is a wonderful collection of classic stories compiled by former Secretary of Education William Bennett. In his introduction to the stories he compiled we read:

> Aristotle wrote that good habits formed at youth make all the difference. And moral education must affirm the central importance of moral example. It has been said that nothing is more influential, more determinate, in a child's life than the moral power of quiet example. For children to take morality seriously they must be in the presence of adults who take morality seriously. And with their own eyes they must see adults taking morality seriously. Along with precept, habit, and example, there is also the need for what we might call moral literacy.

We must address the moral illiteracy of our teens to matters of the soul. The language of story speaks to deeper longings in teens' hearts to know true bravery and love. And we must revive the art of reaching and teaching our kids' hearts with that language. As adults, it must be revived in us as well. We all share the same journey as our young—to discover the brave lovers we were really made to be in our own unfolding story line.

In the following pages you will read stories of love and heroism. As more young people's stories are told that teach powerful Four C lessons, the pickle juice of youth culture will be enriched and fortified in many ways.

The Power of the Powerless: A Story of Character

Christopher de Vinck from *Power of the Powerless*

I was given the book, Power of the Powerless *near the end of our medical ordeal with Michael. Chris de Vinck's experience with his younger brother, Oliver, profoundly affected his life. But his telling of*

Oliver's story profoundly affected my life, and the lives of many readers over the years. He leads us again to that place where, when we enter into the brokenness of another it brings out a rare beauty in us.
Reprinted from The Wall Street Journal, *April 10, 1985. Used by permission.*

I grew up in the house where my brother was on his back in his bed for almost 33 years, in the same corner of his room, under the same window, beside the same yellow walls. Oliver was blind, mute. His legs were twisted. He didn't have the strength to lift his head nor the intelligence to learn anything.

Today I am an English teacher, and each time I introduce my class to the play about Helen Keller, "The Miracle Worker," I tell my students about Oliver. One day, during my first year teaching, a boy in the last row raised his hand and said, "Oh, Mr. de Vinck. You mean he was a vegetable."

I stammered for a few seconds. My family and I fed Oliver. We changed his diapers, hung his clothes and bed linen on the basement line in winter, and spread them out white and clean on the lawn in the summer. I always liked to watch the grasshoppers jump on the pillowcases.

We bathed Oliver. Tickled his chest to make him laugh. Sometimes we left the radio on in his room. We pulled the shade down over his bed in the morning to keep the sun from burning his tender skin. We listened to him laugh as we watched television downstairs. We listened to him rock his arms up and down to make the bed squeak. We listened to him cough in the middle of the night.

"Well, I guess you could call him a vegetable. I called him Oliver, my brother. You would have liked him."

One October day in 1946, while my mother was pregnant with Oliver, her second son, she was overcome by fumes from a leaking coal-burning stove. My oldest brother was sleeping in his crib, which was quite high off the ground so the gas didn't affect him. My father pulled them outside, where my mother revived quickly.

On April 20, 1947, Oliver was born. A healthy-looking, plump, beautiful boy. One afternoon, a few months later, my mother brought Oliver to a window. She held him there in the sun, the bright good sun, and there Oliver looked and looked directly into the sunlight, which was the first moment my mother realized that Oliver was blind.

My parents, the true heroes of this story, learned with the passing months that blindness was only part of the problem. So they brought Oliver to Mount Sinai Hospital in New York for tests to determine the extent of his condition,

The doctor said that he wanted to make it very clear to both my mother and father that there was absolutely nothing that could be done for Oliver. He didn't want my parents to grasp at false hope. "You could place him in an institution," he said. "But," my parents answered, "he is our son. We will take Oliver home, of course." The good doctor answered, "Then take him home and love him."

Oliver grew to the size of a 10-year-old. He had a big chest, a large head. His hands and feet were those of a five-year-old, small and soft. We'd wrap a box of baby cereal for him at Christmas and place it under the tree; pat his head with a damp cloth in the middle of a July heat wave. His baptismal certificate hung on the wall above his head. A bishop came to the house and confirmed him.

Even now, five years after his death from pneumonia on March 12, 1980, Oliver still remains the weakest, most hopeless human being I ever met, and yet he was one of the most powerful human beings I ever met. He could do absolutely nothing except breathe, sleep, eat, and yet he was responsible for action, love, courage, insight.

When I was small my mother would say, "Isn't it wonderful that you can see?" And once she said, "When you go to heaven, Oliver will run to you, embrace you, and the first thing he will say is 'Thank you.'" I remember, too, my mother explaining to me that we were blessed with Oliver in ways that were not clear to her at first.

So often parents are faced with a child who is severely retarded, but who is also hyperactive, demanding or wild, who needs constant care. So many people have little choice but to place their child in an Institution. We were fortunate that Oliver didn't need us to be in his room all day. He never knew what his condition was. We were blessed with his presence, a true presence of peace.

When I was in my early 20s, I met a girl and I fell in love. After a few months I brought her home for dinner to meet my family. When my mother went to the kitchen to prepare dinner, I asked the girl, "Would you like to see Oliver?" for I had told her about my brother. "No," she answered.

Soon after, I met Roe, a lovely girl. She asked me the names of my brothers and sisters. She loved children. I thought she was wonderful. I brought her home after a few months to meet my family. Soon it was time for me to feed Oliver. I remember sheepishly asking Roe if she'd like to see him. "Sure," she said.

I sat at Oliver's bedside as Roe stood and watched over my shoulder. I gave him his first spoonful, his second. "Can I do that?" Roe asked with ease, with freedom, with compassion, so I gave her the bowl, and she fed Oliver one spoonful at a time.

The power of the powerless. Which girl would you marry? Today Roe and I have three children.

Mark's Story: A Story of Conscience

Jan Mezich

> *Jan Mezich is a professional consultant for teachers and has taught teens for many years. She married Steve Mezich, who is a wonderful friend of our family as well. Jan leverages story power in her educator workshops to uplift the principles she teaches.*

Rarely have I met anyone, adult or child, who had such a strong sense of courage to do what is right as Mark. All my students were dear to me, but Mark was one of those never-to-be-forgotten students. Even though twenty-five years have passed, I still remember this quiet, unassuming young man for his forthright display of conscience and courage.

He was in my eighth-grade class at Holy Family School. We were a very close-knit group. I loved every one of my students and they constantly made me realize that the feeling was mutual. We worked hard. I set high academic standards and they seemed to take great pride in meeting and exceeding those standards. Mark had difficulty with reading comprehension, but he worked extra hard to be a good student. We played hard. I coached soccer and softball, umpired games, played first base, chaperoned the ski bus, and organized their bowling league. I remember a close play at home plate. I called Mark out. Mark looked at me and whispered, "You need to go back to umpire school for a refresher." Then he winked at me and returned to the dugout. He always seemed to know how to make me laugh.

I knew my students' mothers and fathers, brothers and sisters. We kept a bulletin board for pictures of family, friends, pets, and special events. By working and playing together our class had formed a very strong bond. We were like a family.

So when ten dollars was stolen from Jessica's coat pocket while it hung in the classroom closet, we were all in shock. It was incredulous that anyone in our homeroom family would even think of doing something dishonest, let alone stealing from someone in our class. In an atmosphere of friendship and trust, we found it difficult to believe that anyone would break that bond. But the money was gone, and no one outside of our group had been in the room. We were saddened and confused.

We held a class meeting, which we did on various occasions to solve problems. The students freely expressed their feeling of disappointment and frustration. It wasn't so much that the ten dollars was the issue, it was that trust had been breached that made them all feel sad.

It was decided that we would set a shoebox for the return of the money out in the hallway and each person in the class would go out of the room one at a time. This would give the opportunity for the thief to return the money anonymously. I told the students that I would put an undisclosed amount of money in the box before anyone went out in the hall. That way no one would be able to accuse the person before him/her of being the one who returned the money. There would be money in the box even when the first person went to the shoebox.

One at a time, the students stepped out of the classroom to visit the shoebox. Because Mark sat in the first desk next to the door, he went first. Each person would spend a minute or two before returning to class. After the last person had a turn, we brought the shoebox back inside and opened it. To everyone's delight, the original money plus the stolen ten dollars was there. Everyone cheered. Whoever had taken the money obviously heard the voice of conscience and returned it. The rest of the day went well and everyone was happy.

After school that day, I was working alone in my classroom when Mark and his friend Scott came in. Kids often came in after school just to hang out or chat. Mark quietly approached me and when we were face to face, he looked me straight in the eye and said, "It was me."

I couldn't speak for a moment because I was trying to clear the lump in my throat. I was so impressed with his honesty. He had been given a chance to return the money anonymously. No one would have ever known who took it. He didn't have to admit his mistake, after all, he had returned the money, and now here he was standing in front of me saying, "It was me."

He went on to say how sorry he was and that he had written a letter of apology to Jessica, which he slipped in her desk so she would find it when she arrived at school the next day.

When I went home after school that day, I left with an enhanced sense of pride in my students and Mark.

Dump Boy: A Story of Compassion
Dump Boy: A Story of Compassion

Philip Gulley, *Hometown Tales*

Philip Gulley is a gifted author and storyteller. He is my friend. He sincerely lives his stories and weaves his words with irony and analogy. He can make you laugh and cry on the same page. In Phil's story about Dump Boy, you will hear the minor chord of one boy's pain harmonize in the heart of another boy.

When I was nine, my parents bought a house on the south edge of town on the way to the landfill. A family's station in life could be measured by its proximity to the dump. We were solid middle class and therefore lived beyond most of the dump's stench. Two or three days a month we could smell it, just enough to remind us that we were rich enough to avoid the smell most of the time but not wealthy enough to escape it altogether.

Down the road from us, dump-ward, lived an old woman and two children. No man. Just that woman and those two kids in a dirty white house down a long, gravel thread of a lane. Where house ended and dump began was barely discernible.

The boy would walk up the road to play with us. When children play, a natural pecking order evolves—over-dog and underdog. He was the underdog, and we over-dogs pointed our barbed arrows of meanness his way. He responded as a cornered dog would, with snarls and bites and lunges, which served to confirm our judgment of him—wild kid, out of control, dump boy.

When things heated up, powerful and potent weapons were unsheathed: "You better leave me alone, or my dad will get you!" This was a weapon he seemed unable to counter. No elevated retort, no "Oh yeah? Well I'll get my dad, and he'll beat up your dad!" Just silence, a turning away, and a walking dump-ward.

I don't remember now how the knowledge came to us, but come to us it did—that his father and mother had been killed and the old woman in the dirty white house was his grandma. I do remember that it had no effect on us; the meanness continued. Despite popular thinking, gentleness is not something we are born with; it is something we are taught, and we had not yet learned it.

The lesson came during a basketball game when an elbow was thrown and dump boy charged my brother—fists flying, rage brimming—right at my brother, who lifted not a hand to defend himself. My brother, who just the week before had chased dump boy back home and hurled rocks, now stood stone-stiff while dump boy battered him. It was an unleashing of fury such as I had never seen, dump boy lashing out at every pain that had ever come his way: the midnight visit of a sheriff's chaplain who explained that Mommy and Daddy wouldn't be coming home, the taunts of children who punished him for his grandma's house, the arrows of meanness which pierce the air and then the soul. Fury raining down.

"Hit him, hit him!" we yelled at my brother. But he raised not a hand, and after a time dump boy tired of the easy kill and went home. We assailed my brother with questions, demanding an explanation for his timidity in battle. He mumbled something about not being able to hit a boy who had lost his parents, that he'd been hit enough as it was.

I did not understand then. And still I struggle with its meaning—how gentleness is never real until fury is aimed our way, how I can be gentle with my infant son but think ill of the eight-item man in the seven-item line at the grocery store. Such little acts turn our hearts from gentleness.

Jesus knew this, knew it not only in his head, but in his heart—that gentleness, of all the fruits, is the hardest to cultivate. How strong our tendency to return the blow, to hurl the rock, to call the name. Until our hearts are likewise broken. Why is it that gentleness must necessarily spring from rocky soil, from hardship, from ground sowed with tears?

One day, I prayed to the Lord to teach me gentleness and sat about, waiting for good to happen. Instead, God showed me sorrow and thus began my education.

Dump boy moved away the next year. I haven't seen him since. Don't even know if he's alive. I hope his life is sweet, that he married well, that tiny children crowd his lap and call him sweeter names than we did.

Anne: A Story of Courage

Anne: A Story of Courage

Reprinted by permission of Ina Hughes.

This is a story about a story. Goodness and truth have a knack for doing such things, to be preserved and passed down in many ways—to be admired from many different angles. It is the story of a teenage girl whose bravery helped her to protect the beautiful garden in her soul. The Diary of Anne Frank has influenced millions over decades. One little girl with an eternal-sized heart was lifted above her fears by gripping the power of goodness and truth—her words of hope have lifted many others.

Her real name was Annelies Marie, but people called her Anne. Except her mother. Sometimes when her mother was feeling especially impatient or sentimental, she called Anne by her real name.

Like most teenagers of any name or place, Anne was in love with life—one minute humming and giggling, then when somebody looked at her wrong or a dark thought came out from the corners of her mind, she fought tears and bit her lip. She wondered what it would be like to be in love, and took up almost a whole page in her diary when she got her first kiss. She wasn't precocious or brilliant. Her grades in school were average, at best. She was not beautiful—but she had spirit and spunk and could smile on the outside, and while those things did not save her life, they made her immortal.

Anne Frank.

It's odd, isn't it, that one of the bestsellers of all times was not written by a "writer" or a great "teacher" or a world leader. It was written by a teenage girl hiding in an attic.

Anne had two birthdays in that attic. She was barely 13 the summer afternoon in 1942 when her family gathered up a few things and walked in the pouring rain across Amsterdam to a warehouse above her father's grocery business. On August 1, 1944—two months after her 15th birthday—Nazi police burst through the door. Yanking open drawers, ripping mattresses, the police stuffed jewelry in their pockets and looked for hidden money.

Then, shoving Anne and her family down the steps, into waiting cars, they drove off. No one immediately noticed the red-checkered diary left behind.

Anne was 16 when she came down with typhus in Bergen-Belsen. Her mother died of exhaustion, her sister of malnutrition. Only her father was found alive, liberated by Russians at Auschwitz. Anne never knew all this. She died three months before her 17th birthday.

Nor did she have any idea that years later, over 2,000 young people would march in the rain to Bergen-Belsen to place flowers on the mass grave into which she had been thrown like a piece of garbage.

"[No one] will be interested in the unbosoming of a 13-year-old schoolgirl," she writes in the first pages of her diary. She was wrong. That diary is translated into over 30 languages, her name a household word. The attic on the Prinsengracht Canal in Amsterdam is now a museum.

A week after the Franks' arrest, a family friend found the diary and, after the war, gave it to Anne's father. In 1947, though turned down by two Dutch publishing houses, it came out under the title *Diary of a Young Girl*. Ever since, people have turned to that attic prison where the only sunlight came from the unquenchable spirit of a teenage girl whom teachers had found average. Through this dreamy adolescent, we watch the world grow dark, fear moving through every aspect of life like a cancer on the loose.

We know from the outset how it will all end, but Anne sees things differently. Even as the news sputtering in over the radio grows worse and worse, Anne continues to write happy stories about elves, bears, and an old dwarf. Even as she sits crammed up in the secret corner of a world gone mad, she talks about playing Ping-Pong and how good the sun feels on her face. Even after she loses one of her many private bouts with encroaching loneliness, she says she knows in her heart that people are basically kind, and that no matter what happens, good will win out.

Did it? Will it again?

A hundred years before Anne Frank wrote in her diary, an old British scholar, sitting in his soft leather chair and enjoying a good cigar, wrote these immortal words: "The pen is mightier than the sword." It was a teenage girl who not only proved it, but went one better:

In the long run, the sharpest weapon of all is a kind and gentle spirit.

The following stories were written by kids. In their own words, each shares the lessons learned and blessings received by helping other.

What I've Learned by Helping Others

The following story reflects the wisdom and capacity of young people to wrestle with and resolve real life issues with God's goodness as the foundation of their hope. The story is excerpted from Things I've Learned Lately, *an insightful and wonderfully written book by seventeen-year-old Danae Jacobson.*

Life Is Unfair, but God Is Good

When someone I love is hurting, I always find myself asking, *Why?*

For example, it doesn't make sense that my beautiful, blond baby cousin, AvonLeah, was born blind and with severe disabilities. As I write this, she is a little over six months old, yet she may never be able to do anything more that what she can right now, mentally or physically. When I think about the life she will probably lead, I can't help but ask God, *Why?*

I know God tells us that there is a time and a season for everything. But why does there have to be a time for bad things? Why was there a time for the Holocaust? Why the Ku Klux Klan? Why a time for Columbine? Why did my friend try to kill himself? Why are there little girls without daddies, and why are there little girls with daddies who hurt them? Why do freak accidents kill innocent people? The list is endless. *Why?*

It seems so wrong when someone has more than his or her "*fair* share" of heartache and tragedy. *My best friend* has had *just* about the hardest year I could imagine. Seeing the pain she's gone through, the pain that has taken her family and tried to destroy it, makes me cry for her. She's only seventeen. Why should she have to go through all that?

As I struggle with these issues, I wonder if everybody reaches this point eventually—the point when you realize that life truly is unfair. This is not the kind of unfairness you screamed about when you were four and didn't get a red Popsicle like your sister. This is the kind of unfairness you scream about when you get a phone call at 1:47 in the morning telling you that your friend was killed in an car accident with a drunk driver.

Bad things can happen to anyone for seemingly no reason. You can ask why as many times as you want, and you'll never really get the answer you're looking for.

But lately I'm beginning to wonder if *Why?* is the right question, if *What now?* might be a better one. No matter what bad things happen to those I love, to me, or to anyone in the world, I know that God has not left us alone. God still cares. God is good. Only he can bring something good out of something awful in people's lives—if they're willing to cooperate with him.

Recently I read *Night* by Elie Wiesel, the famous Holocaust survivor. The things he saw and lived through in a German concentration camp as a fifteen-year-old boy were horrific, and they *destroyed* the faith and lives of many men three times his age. The word *senseless* seems to describe what happened perfectly. Yet when I consider what Wiesel has done with that nightmare, what necessary, righteous outrage his books have inspired, I'm amazed at how much good came out of the evil he endured.

My dad always says this about bad times: "You have two options. One, you can complain about the bad things in your life that you can't change, making yourself and those around you miserable. Or two, you can take the bad things that happen and try to discover what good God can bring out of them."

He's right. We've all seen people who go through life taking option number one. They spend so much time complaining and asking *Why?* that they get bitter and miss the beauty of life altogether.

I want to make the second choice, which is the one my aunt and uncle have made. As I've spent time with them and the rest of their kids, I've discovered that they don't see AvonLeah's disabilities as this horrible thing that has happened. They see my cousin as a precious gift and a wonderful blessing. And I have to agree. I've seen people in my family, in my school, and in the community come together around her in a way they never would have otherwise.

Sometimes when I hold AvonLeah and she smiles up at me, for a second I forget she is blind, and I imagine she can see me smiling back at her.

Sometimes I wonder if we're not all a little bit like her. Right now, on this side of heaven, we're often blinded to the good in our lives by the bad things that happen. We suffer and we feel alone. But all the while God is holding us close, smiling at us, wanting us to experience his blessing and perfect plan for our lives, and hoping we are aware of his love.

Have courage for the great sorrows of life and
patience for the small ones
and when you have laboriously accomplished
your daily task, go to sleep in peace. God is awake.

Victor Hugo

And we know that in all things God works
for the good of those who love him,
who have been called according to his purpose.

Romans 8:28

What I've Learned by Helping Others

What I've Learned by Helping Others

by Ashley Lowery

During the last year, my grandma was diagnosed with sarcoma cancer. Her name is Cristina Himes. She has been one of the most inspiring persons in my life.

The reason I am writing this paper is because I believe that what the Sparrow Clubs are doing for kids is something that is good for families. Could you imagine being the parent of a child that has cancer? It was hard for me to discover that my grandma had cancer. I spent long hours in my room crying, wondering if she would make it through surgery.

My grandma underwent surgery on March 14, 2000. I was at school at the time and all through the day the tears came off and on. It was a day I will never forget. Today the cancer has returned in her lung and liver. From what I know and have heard about sarcoma cancer, it is very aggressive, and once you have it, it is extremely hard to get rid of. I did a report for language arts on this subject and I feel that it is important for people to understand this is what can happen. In a life that has meant so much to me, to my family, and even to the people who know her, how could God let this happen?

Today her back spasms have come back and she is in more pain than ever. It is hard to think about her condition. Everyone who knows her loves her. She is generous, very loving, and full of care. She has been an inspiration for me to show my care for her and to others around me. If it were not for her condition in life right now, I would have taken her love for granted, but since I am seeing her in her last days, I have felt the love she has for my family and me. If it wasn't for this love I don't know if I would be the same person that I am today. I never want to forget this love that has meant so much to me.

What I've Learned by Helping Others

What I've Learned by Helping Others

by Mandi Puch

What I have done is small in many ways, but not the way that I see it. I look at what I have done for others and I believe that I have made an impact. One thing that I remember doing is helping my dear friend Larry. I met Larry in the seventh grade, at a Seattle middle school. He looked different, and he sure acted different than any other person I had ever met. He had a warm personality and a "quirky" sense of humor. But what I remember happened in the eighth grade, nearly a year after our meeting.

We were down in a local dance club that we went to on our Friday nights. Now one thing that you must know about Larry was that he had a reputation of being a troublemaker. He knew how to get in trouble and he knew how to get out of it when he wanted to. But back to the dance club … It was a typical Friday night. Everyone was hot and sweaty but everyone was having fun. Larry had been there about as long as I had been there, if not a bit longer. Halfway through the night the police came down. We all had a surprised reaction for it seemed like they were looking on the sign-in sheets to get someone. Over the loud speaker, the music became quiet, and D.J. yelled, "Larry please go to the front." Larry was scared. Everyone thought that he was in trouble, for vandalism or even drugs. But in the morning I got a phone call from my teacher, Mrs. Goodman. I answered the phone. What I had heard was so shocking that I almost fell on the floor.

I had discovered the truth; it was not trouble. It was tragedy. His mother, Tracey, had died. How she died I will not say, but it was a very hard way to die. Larry came to school that Monday. It was very hard to be around him at first, for fear of saying a wrong comment.

I sat in the office with Larry for about a half hour before anyone said anything. But once we both got started, I started asking him questions about his mother and I started getting answers. We both started talking, and I learned about his emotions. About how he felt now that his mother was no longer here physically, but only in his heart.

When I helped Larry, not only did I learn about his emotions but I learned about my own, too. If I had not had that conversation with Larry about his mother I would not be half the person that I am today, and I would not be as emotionally strong either. Larry was able to move on, able to keep his mother living in his heart and in the hearts of the ones that he loved and that loved her as well. Talking to him, I learned so much about emotions and the human being. I learned that everyone has feelings. But depending on the person, some are more sensitive to others, and after something like this, they are not ever the same.

What I've Learned by Helping Others

by Damian Noske

I had a best friend that died in a house fire and I'll tell how we met and said good bye. One day my mom was looking for a house, and my mom met someone named Robbie, and we moved in with her. She and my mom have been best friends ever since. My friend Andy and I would stay at each other's house every weekend. He and I would hide from his little brothers Jeremy, Brandon, and Dakota. They wouldn't be able to find us for at least an hour. That's a long time for being nine and ten years old. One day I was going hunting. Dave, the man who was taking me hunting, said I had to get up at four in the morning. Before we left we heard some sirens. Then we left and we saw some smoke near my friend's house, but I didn't know it was coming from my friend's house. When Dave and I got back, my mom came up to me, and she was crying, and I said "What's wrong?" She said "Andy has died," and I stood there in shock. Dave said "I'm sorry, I'm truly sorry." I didn't cry because I was in shock but I said, "No, it can't be." And then my mom said "Come on. Let's go inside." We sat on the couch and talked about it, and I said "It can't be. Why? Why? It just can't be."

The next morning I was sitting in the rocking chair on the front porch and my mom said "What are you doing?" and I said "I'm thinking about what Andy and I would be doing if Andy was alive."

At the funeral you could see Andy and Brandon's mom crying, and I was heartbroken so I gave her a hug, and that made her feel a lot better. And after that we gave her clothes. We gave her shoes and we gave her love and hope. And now she does daycare and we go there. That's how I helped Andy's family. If I ever need help, someone might help me in return. Kids can make a difference in the world.

What I've Learned by Helping Others

by Linnea Thomassen

Walking down the sidewalk to recess, I saw Jeffery, a young man in a wheelchair. He had brown hair and was about three and one half feet tall. He was afraid of almost every kid in the school. One of his wheels was stuck in a rut. Some of my friends began to laugh. He said, "Help me, please!" in a way that I will never forget. I told my friends "That's not right, stop it." They giggled and chorused together, "Linnea has a boyfriend."

I didn't care. I helped move Jeff's chair out of the rut. At recess he asked me if I wanted to play basketball. So I did. For the next few days I sat with him at lunch, played with him at recess, and we became very good friends.

Then one morning he didn't come to school. I asked the teacher where he was. She said, "He's having surgery on both of his legs, and it might help his walking abilities"

"Oh," I said. "Do you know when he'll be back?"

"No," she responded.

I went back to my desk. Three days later he was back with two casts on his legs.

"Your boyfriend back?" some of my former friends asked. I ignored them. I was thinking to myself, *I bet you guys couldn't go in for surgery and come back to school after three days.*

Soon after that I got some people to hang out with him. He became a little popular after that.

It's great to help others! I've learned that helping others is fun, and it is a good thing to do!

What I've Learned by Helping Others

by Erik Hisel

I've learned many things by helping others. The best part I like about helping others is that it makes that person happy. The story I'm about to tell is a good example of what happens when you help others.

When I was in fourth grade I was called to help others in math. I didn't want to, but I did. There was one kid who was really stumped. When I was done helping him, he was zooming through his problems. I was proud and he was happy. It lifted my spirit to help as much as possible.

By helping people you learn that some people need help and not all people know everything. Helping comes from the heart and soul, not the brain. This is what I've learned by helping people.

What I've Learned by Helping Others

What I've Learned by Helping Others

by Jacob Kurzer

My name is Jacob. I go to school at Amity Creek. I'm six years old. I'm in kindergarten.

One day a man came to our school, and he told us about a little girl that was sick. Her name is Ashley. She's sick with cancer in her arm tissue. That made me feel sort of bad because she's sick. I would not like to be sick like that. The man told us about a way to raise money for Ashley and her family. If you had one hundred dollars for Ashley then it would become two hundred dollars for Ashley. If we did work in the community for an hour then we would earn ten dollars of Sparrow cash that goes to Ashley.

When I first heard I wanted to go right to my bank and get my money and go right to the man that came to our school and say, "This money will go to Ashley, please." First I gave five dollars, but later when my aunt sent me some money, I gave ten more. When I gave five, it made ten and when I gave ten it made twenty. Ten and twenty make thirty, so I gave thirty dollars to Ashley. That made me feel good in my heart.

I do lots of work, but I also get lots of stuff back. I have done yard work for the people that can't do it as well. It makes me feel good because I'm giving to others. When you do this work you're into lots of action and it helps your muscles.

There was somebody that I used to visit that had some kind of disease, and he died with that disease. He used to live at Harmony House. It's a home for people that can't do things for themselves. I'm going to go back there and help people play games. I think that will make me feel good because I'm helping others that can't do stuff for themselves.

I get to help Ashley *and* other people because helping other people is how I earn money for Ashley. I like what I have already, that I have all that I need and I don't need anymore. Learning about Ashley and doing all this work helps to show me that I can help others and be who I am. I like to help others and I get pretty much a lot back when I give to others.

(And my brother says, "I like getting money for Ashley.")

Chapter Nine
The Fifth C: Communities of Sanctuary

*Public rivers of goodness grow
From springs of love in every soul.*

C ommunity is the Fifth C. It grows from the Four Cs that precede it. Love is the chemistry of healthy community. It is good pickle juice, something our souls were made to be immersed in. It is sanctuary— protecting, providing, nurturing, empowering, and disarming all at once. From a mother's love for her unborn child, to hospitality for a stranger, to paying fair taxes—it is doing things God's way. A religious expert once confronted Jesus with this question, " 'Teacher, which is the most important commandment in the law of Moses?' Jesus replied, 'You must love the Lord your God with all your heart, all your soul, and all your mind.' This is the first and greatest commandment. A second is equally important: 'Love your neighbor as yourself' " (Matt. 22:37–40, NLT).

Jesus was the one who went around healing hurting people, visiting with sinners, and teaching unheard of things like, "If you are slapped on the right cheek, turn the other, too. If you are ordered to court and your shirt is taken from you, give your coat, too. If a soldier demands that you carry his gear for a mile, carry it two miles. Give to those who ask, and don't turn away from those who want to borrow" (Matt. 5:39–42, NLT). Maybe the expert should have known that Jesus would say we love God by loving people and love people by loving God.

Love requires little legislation. Courts, regulations, and government bureaucracy can never replace the simple effectiveness of conscientious people who live by the Golden Rule. People who live the law of love through the Four Cs best serve their community. Every individual has a profound place in community under God's authority. But every person must be content and committed to simply work, rest, grow, live, and love in her or his place. Community is not defined by Four B traits yielding the Four Powers of position, property, popularity, or prestige. Ambitiously climbing the ladder on the social hierarchy above others has nothing to do with community. There is no such thing as higher or lower place in community. Higher positions of power are only indications of greater obligations to serve—not to self-indulge.

Politicians who are community-minded people earn respect like good doctors do, not like media celebrities do. It was the great statesman John Adams who wrote, "Upon common theaters, indeed, the applause of the audience is of more importance to the actors than their own approbation. But upon the stage of life, while conscience claps, let the world hiss! On the contrary if conscience disapproves, the loudest applauses of the world are of little value." It is the desire of a servant leader to deliver care that makes him or her trusted and effective in the long run, not the applause meters of opinion polls, staying on the charts, or doing whatever it takes to get voted back into office.

Community goes beyond geography. It is a series of seven widening circles of relationship, or sanctuaries, that surround us. Like a ripple effect, these circles begin intimately tight and gradually expand to become very wide—as wide as the world of all God's children. There are great distinctions in how relationships operate within each circle, but they are all threaded together by the law of love and founded upon the principles of truth, goodness, justice, and mercy. Like growth rings inside a tree, each circle is a sanctuary of protection. Our Four Cs grow and expand, absorbing love and expressing love from the innermost circles outwardly. And every tree is a safe haven for the smallest sparrow.

Kids who are immersed in the pickle juice of these seven sanctuaries or healthy communities are most likely to recover from painful tragedies, have their hearts disarmed of hostilities, and be empowered for life by love.

Sanctuary #1: The Mother's Womb

In June of 1995, I wrote an article for *Ladies' Home Journal* titled, "The Purest Love." Barbara Barton's story tells of a mother who chose to forego aggressive treatment for leukemia to save the lives of her unborn twins. She postponed a bone-marrow transplant and chose a harder, more painful, and risky regimen for her treatment—all to give her babies every chance for life and health. Her babies lived. Barbara did not. A woman's suffering body became a sanctuary for her children, born in her choice to sacrifice her life for theirs. This is an illustration of God's love.

The first most intimate place of community is the womb of a mother. A mother's womb is a sacred place—a reserve for the sanctity of married love and then for the sanctity of new life. This points to something significant—how God connects commitment and love to life itself. The womb is a perfect model of the world's safest place to be, in God's design that is; the place of highest love protecting the most helpless being.

When I taught high school health I had a set of life-sized fetal models for my classes to see. I didn't lecture about pro-life versus pro-choice positions. My students could pull the plastic replicas out of their womb-like molds. They could hold the "babies," as they intuitively call them, in the palm of their hand. The smallest model represented a stage when mothers likely wouldn't even know they were pregnant. Teens are often surprised to learn that their total nature is locked into their genetic makeup, their DNA, at the moment of conception. From that instant forward everything depends on nurture—or the sanctuary of another's love—to reach our highest natural potential in God's design. Even though the conditions continually change, we all need the secret sanctuary of other people's love to bring out the best in us. Especially as an unborn child.

Years ago, my wife, Kristi, and I took in a baby from the hospital and kept him for four months. We had known his teenage mother, Samantha, as a student in my school. She was a poor performer, had a low sense of self-respect, and was sexually exploited by boys. Even though she was pregnant several times, Samantha chose the sanctuary of adoption for her children. And even though she needed real help at a soul-level, her choices not only protected small lives but also provided childless and loving couples with the joy of family. I applaud her courage, especially when many kids are scared into making convenient decisions without understanding the ultimate cost and loss. Abortion has become an insanely lucrative industry. But legalization cannot stop love from convicting consciences to protect life like Samantha did.

God will forgive women and couples who have chosen abortion. But the soul remains deeply scarred. Many women are finding emotional healing in loving Christian support groups for post-abortion trauma. The womb is the first circle of sanctuary. It is a community for the smallest, weakest, and most innocent of all human beings—the unborn child. Kids today must first be protected from the tyranny of an abortion industry that has grown from new morality legislation. Our laws make a powerful statement about the inherent value we place on life itself.

Sanctuary #2: The Marriage Relationship

Sanctuary #2: The Marriage Relationship

A husband and wife committed for life is the second most intimate community of sanctuary for kids. My parents were married for fifty-four years before my dad passed away. Mom and dad's commitment to each other continues to leave a legacy of what married sanctuary could and should be for five sons, their wives, eighteen grandchildren and six great-grandchildren. The fidelity of marriage is irreplaceable as a sanctuary for kids. Children must be taught to stay in the circle of this sanctuary by honoring their parents.

Our pastor gave Kristi and me several sessions of wise counsel before we took our vows. He told us that marriage is like being stranded in a leaky dingy at sea. He said many couples tie another boat behind them called divorce. It's an alternative. But after years of continued bailing and work, divorce can look like a luxury yacht in comparison to their dingy. What couples don't realize is that the divorce boat often leaks worse than the dingy. He said it's best not to have the "divorce" word in our vocabulary. It has been good advice. Kristi and I celebrated our twenty-second anniversary this summer.

The biblical judge named Samson was enticed, captured, and blinded by an affair with a woman named Delilah. Airbrushed media images, infatuations, and youthful passion capture and blind many men and women in the process of destroying marriages. In the same way that happiness is attracted to the sanctuary of good character, romance is attracted and protected in the sanctuary of faithful and sacrificial love in marriage.

Legislation is weakening the sanctuary of marriage. No-fault divorce makes the institution very fickle. Divorce rates are staggering. Broken children fall in the wake of broken promises. They often blame themselves for their parents' breakup. Family legacies and the lifelong commitment of two parents strengthen children's souls. Other attacks on the traditional institution of marriage surprise us. Same sex marriages fly in the face of natural love, logic, and long-term consequences. Homosexuality separates married love and the act of sex from the potential of creating life. Even if it's mandated by new morality, state-endorsed homosexual marriages will never be natural or right. The marriage institution is the second-most intimate community of sanctuary that must be protected for the well-being of kids.

Dr. Brenda Hunter is a psychologist, author, and passionate defender of the mother-child bond. She has written a remarkable book packed with research about the positive impact stay-at-home moms have on their children. It is titled *Home by Choice.* Her dedication page resonates in my heart; it's written to mothers, "who have chosen, at no little sacrifice, to be at home with their children." She continues, "I applaud you for your courage in a culture that is hostile to your choice. I support you in your willingness to put your children's well-being ahead of any career advancement. And I uphold your conviction that you are the best person to raise your child. You are the unsung heroines of this century." And I agree wholeheartedly. In her book, Dr. Hunter points out the irreplaceable role and importance of mothering. She shows how even the most minor face-to-face interactions of mother and child matter. Her love builds trust and helps set the stage for healthy emotional development.

Kristi and I have limped along financially over the years. Even if she only earned a modest wage, we could have paid for lots of stuff and taken many vacations in the time she has spent making our home and schooling our kids. But whenever we consider her taking on an outside job to help pay bills, we lose interest. We know the richness of relationship and the deposits being made into our kids' souls will eventually pay off in greater ways than can be materially measured. Home and family life is designed by God to be the tightest circle of healthy socialization. It is the birthplace of deference in our souls—where keeping the peace with mom, dad, brothers, and sisters helps us to learn empathy, respect, obedience, submission, courtesy, and duty. It is where we see, up close and center stage, the consequences of our choices on the well-being of others.

Real love does not hopscotch over the family community for the sake of work community. That is not love but ambition. It is out of place, in the surface-level, and unbecoming of God's design.

In 1580 Montaigne wrote in his *Essays,* "Many a man has been a wonder to the world, whose wife and valet have seen nothing in him that was even remarkable. Few men have been admired by their servants." I am continually cautioned in my conscience about chasing a vision of changing the world while failing to see what my family sees in me. I can conquer great things in the world's eyes, but in the light of God's glory, being a brave lover to my family is truly a more heroic story.

True community calls us to care for our family. Home is where welfare is most effectively and efficiently administrated as well. "A friend is always loyal, and a brother is born to help in the time of need" (Prov. 17:17, NLT). There is a special bond of affection and accountability in blood relationships. Even the church cannot replace this calling of the family. Early Christians were shirking their duties and presuming upon the church to take care of their needy family members. The Apostle Paul exhorted them, "But those who won't care for their own relatives, especially those living in the same household, have denied what we believe. Such people are worse than unbelievers" (1Tim. 5:8, NLT).

The most difficult place to exercise our Four Cs is at home, taking care of our own family. But it is a sanctuary that is well worth protecting and providing for. The impact of this community is one that neither church, career, or government can replace.

Sanctuary #4: The Church Community

When I hear the word sanctuary, I often associate it with churches. We own a reprinted edition of the 1828 Noah Webster dictionary. One of the definitions of sanctuary is "a sacred asylum." Places of asylum stem from ancient times. These were religious places of refuge where known debtors and criminals could, as Webster defines, "shelter themselves from justice, and from which they cannot be taken without sacrilege." Ancient Jews, too, had cities of refuge. Historically, criminals could find protection in church sanctuaries.

Outside of family, churches are the primary places of soul-healing sanctuary in communities. Churches are hospitals for sinners, not museums for saints. They are places of refuge where undeserving people find mercy, grace, and restoration for their souls. God's people have heart-gifts to build sanctuary in the lives of others. And godly communities have divine power to bring the resources of heaven to bear on the world's needs.

Tom Sabens and his wife, Jane, are on the board of directors for Sparrow Clubs. Tom is the senior pastor of Tablerock Fellowship, a large church in southern Oregon. His facility is bursting at its seams, and plans are underway for a building expansion project. I was visiting his church one Sunday and it seemed clear to me why God is blessing this fellowship with rapidly expanding borders. That morning, I heard Tom reaffirm the vision and mission of the church. It is not about "buildings, bucks, and bodies" as Tom said. It is about getting outside the four walls and practically reaching people in the community with God's love. The work of that church is about building a big enough sanctuary to contain their entire community, and that doesn't start with a building project. It means having a vision for expanding the walls of our faith and love to build in the hearts of people.

A big part of that vision is helping teens to catch a vision too. Under the leadership of youth pastor C.J. McPhail and his wife, Lindsay, Table Rock started a Sparrow Club. Hundreds of teens adopted a sparrow, a local three-year-old boy named Tanner who suffered a rare bleeding disorder. The youth collectively did over 256 hours of service by cleaning a run-down cemetery in their community. Their efforts earned $2,560 in Sparrow cash, sponsored by the local Airport Chevrolet dealership, to help the boy and his family. But the sparrow project did more than raise money. I believe it raised the hopes of these teens to look beyond their own lives. It gave them a "connecting experience" as they reached out to meet the needs of a child. They became conduits of God's love.

I was there when Tanner's mom introduced him to the kids one night at youth group. God poured compassion into many teens as they came forward, kneeled, prayed, and wept for God to touch the life of their sparrow child. It was real stuff. Later, C.J. candidly shared with me what most youth pastors desperately desire. Fun, games, music, facilities, and entertainment may get teens to show up to youth group, but have no power to change hearts. Most youth pastors ache to see kids' hearts anointed with God's love the way C.J.'s group experienced.

Not long after those events, with the blessing of Tom and the entire pastoral staff at Tablerock Fellowship, C.J. became a fulltime Sparrow Club staff member in Medford, Oregon. C.J. and Lindsay have taken youth teams on mission trips to Mexico for years. Now his mission is getting outside the four walls of the church sanctuary and bringing the sanctuary of God's love into his area schools.

Sanctuary #5: The School and Neighborhood

Churches can be suitable substitutes for family. But the public circle outside the church family can really begin to feel relationally cold and distant. The seven circles of sanctuary have different kinds and levels of intimacy. But the circles also quantify numbers of relationships to manage too.

Generally, the smaller the circle
>   the fewer people are in it
>   the better we can be known within it
>   the better we can know others who are in it
>   the more we will have in common with the others in it
>   and the greater potential impact our behaviors have to either help or
harm others at a deeper soul level.

During a teacher staff meeting this quote was projected on a screen, "Particularly distressing are conflicts with persons in ongoing, non-family relationships because these relationships have continuity and yet usually have insufficient intimacy and understanding to prevent arguments from being perceived as a major threat." The words came from an educational specialist named Charles Blondino. The point of the discussion that followed was simply how to be good neighbors as co-workers at school. People are quirky. Our different goals, desires, tastes, opinions, interests, and ambitions can quickly lead to differences. As our circles of relationship widen, our capacity to understand other people's immediate feelings—and the emotional context that causes those feelings—lessens.

When Michael was hospitalized with leukemia, I was definitely carrying some heavy emotional baggage with me to school. Though I tried, I was so consumed with needs in my smaller circles that I had difficulty empathizing with others in wider ones. For instance, I remember a time when I had just returned from a few days' absence because of a difficult bout Michael had in the hospital. A fellow physical education teacher approached me before school and vented a complaint about how my substitute failed to stack the pickle-ball paddles properly in the storage room. Believe me, it was difficult for me to feel her pain! I felt like I was holding back a volcano inside me, while she stood on my crater's rim and taunted me by tossing in a firecracker. I battled against the urge to vent back at her. I almost blew up. What I didn't understand at the time is that everybody's pain feels like a volcano to them. And only our empathy and compassion have the power to drain it positively. When we vent back on someone else, it's only tossing more firecrackers into their volcano. But when we get into their shoes and feel their pain, we disarm explosions and release them to understand our pain without defensiveness as well.

In retrospect, I now understand that it was only my own emotional and spiritual immaturity that made me want to vent back instead of empathize.

Young people today have much inner-circle pain and lack emotional maturity to deal with it in healthy ways. And we wonder why they're venting. They're being pushed out of their homes into school and neighborhood circles that lack intimacy and empathy by parents who have their own inner circle relationship pains in their marriage. Single parents struggle to survive financially and raise their families. Kids are adrift in social oceans without anchors of love to secure them. But schools with small, caring circles like adaptive PE where kids share in helping each other are sanctuaries for broken hearts.

As adults, and especially for followers of Christ, what matters on the grand scale of life is not so much the weightiness of what we feel, but rather our capacity to carry our load and still care about the loads of others in all circles of relationship. Galatians 6:2 says, "Bear one another's burdens, and thus fulfill the law of Christ" (NASB). When our souls are in alignment with the principles of God, we experience the power of God to help us be burden-bearers and pain-drainers.

School and neighborhood sanctuary is, as Dameon so deeply desired, a safe place. It's a place where kids can heal and help and know they won't be harmed. It's a place where every kid matters. God especially cares about the pickle juice of culture that immerses kids. The Four Cs of young people change the chemistry of school culture and neighborhoods back into the communities God intends them to be.

Sanctuary #6: The Business Community

The business community is a sanctuary where our Four Bs are put to good work. When they are governed by a person's Four Cs, brawn, beauty, brains, and bank accounts are tools that bring productivity and prosperity into our communities. God's people have gifts and talents. But principles of fair and free trade weave the assets and needs of people together in wonderful ways. In good economy, two parties can profit from one transaction. Each gains something they value above what they traded. Profits motivate hard work, and work produces more goods. More trades occur, production demand is higher, and more jobs are created. Working communities are happy communities.

Unfortunately, government can invade the sanctuary of free trade. Often it is necessary for a small amount of taxes. But over-taxation government is like a monster that devours individual incentive to take risks and start businesses that create jobs. By taxing too much, government destroys the desire of people to work hard and be productive. Big government is like the greedy farmer who cut open the goose to get its golden eggs.

On the other hand, big business can become a greedy monster too. Owners can become so powerful and blinded by self-interest and short-term profits, that they destroy the communities that provide their workforce and the markets that purchase their products. Many big businesses, however, have generous philanthropic branches that give back to the communities. Those endowments have allowed the communities to grow and flourish.

We often don't think the laws of love operate in business communities, but they do. The words of Jesus can turn any community into a sanctuary, "It is more blessed to give than to receive" (Acts 20:35, NASB).

Sanctuary #7: The Government

Awhile ago Kristi stood behind a man in a nice suit buying gourmet steaks with food stamps. After paying for her groceries, she walked out to see the same man drive out of the parking lot in an expensive sports car. Today, aggressive government programs assume much responsibility to care for families that could and should fend for themselves. Government is the least intimate of all communities. That is why it is best suited for the business of justice and not mercy. For that reason it is the least effective and least efficient in meeting the real needs of people. Government is the most costly and least effective and least efficient way of taking care of people problems. And it is the most easily taken advantage of by people like that guy in the grocery store.

Socialism and big government programs are only necessary when smaller communities are not living by the laws of love, where individual citizens are not conscientious and do not exercise their other three Cs. Government is necessary for some public goods like utilities, roads, and a few other shared services. They are most important to protect our borders with a strong defense against acts of war. But government power grows in proportion to the collective weakness of its citizens' Four Cs.

The framers of our nation's constitution clearly presumed upon the power of God to help them form a more perfect union. The phrase "one nation under God" simply means that no person or groups of people ever have the right to usurp our Creator's moral absolutes from guiding our legislative acts. The real backbone of our government is our Judeo-Christian ethics that preserve democractic vote, provide for representative leadership, and promote religious freedom. Our nation's biblical underpinnings keep the machinery of many different people of diverse faiths and backgrounds working together in peace and prosperity. Our constitution is a piece of paper that points to the importance of the Four Cs in the hearts of our people. Its main purposes are to empower individuals who are guided by natural moral law and to limit a government that hungers for power.

The God of Good Community

About 2,000 years ago God visited this planet that he made. He came in person, but didn't mix much with the Four B crowd—no brainy degrees or elite education, no brawny political clout, no outward appeal or beauty, and no financial nest egg or bank accounts. God was just passing' through this world with a higher purpose in mind. He came to meet the deepest human need. To give hope for a life that lies beyond this life. He came to reconnect man to a relationship with himself and with a heavenly lifestyle of love.

A few years ago the "WWJD—What Would Jesus Do?" theme became a powerful and popular movement in Christian youth culture. Jesus exercised his Four Cs perfectly when he walked through humanity. The actions of Jesus speak most eloquently to the hearts of kids. Doing things the way that Jesus did them is the ideal example for young people to follow in developing their Four Cs. But the Son of God didn't just visit his Creation 2,000 years ago to merely model how to live a good life. He came to do something that is impossible for people to do. As the bravest lover of all, Jesus willingly laid down his life to pay for our sins against God. We were helpless to earn God's favor, but Jesus' body and blood became the only trustworthy bridge across the eternal chasm of separation that our sins caused. He took care of our deepest need and disarmed the highest hostility in man's heart against God. Jesus is the reconnection to God's deep, unconditional wellspring of love for any who will simply take the trust fall into his arms for salvation. God does not force the reconnection to his love upon us. We are invited into this powerful love relationship and must respond by opening our hearts' doors of faith. As the risen Christ said, "Look! Here I stand at the door and knock. If you hear me calling and open the door, I will come in, and we will share a meal as friends" (Rev. 3:20, NLT). He is the God of disarmed hearts and healthy communities indeed.

Appendix One

SPARROW CLUBS™ … FIND YOUR WINGS.

Dameon was a lonely, struggling junior high student who knew rejection well. He became the inspiration for an entire community when he cleaned out his life savings of twelve five-dollar bills to help pay for a life-saving but uninsured bone marrow transplant for Michael—a little boy with leukemia.

This generosity of spirit initiated an outreach of teens at Kamiakin Junior High in Kirkland, Washington who helped raise $227,000 in four weeks to save Michael's life. From this story of hope and strength in hearts of these heroic youth, Sparrow Clubs was born, an organization committed to empowering kids to help kids in medical need.

WHERE HOPE TAKES WING

Since its inception in 1995 as a youth-based 501 (c) (3) educational charity, the Sparrow Clubs organization has helped children in medical crisis through the work of thousands of young people. Sparrow Clubs do more than just provide financial and emotional support for the families of these critically ill children. They help kids like Dameon find their wings through giving, expressing compassion, and experiences in serving others.

Today's youth are the most emotionally detached, isolated, and angry generation ever. It's critically important to provide our youth with experiences that give purpose, teach compassion, and instill character, dignity, and community. Dameon's compassionate gift is an example of a hurting kid wanting to help. The resounding outpouring to save Michael proves that purposelessness and rage can be diffused and redirected when a local child needs help. Kids become recognized as heroes by showing empathy … identifying and sharing God's love in practical ways. Sparrow Clubs is a wonderful vehicle for **kids helping kids.**

No one understands kids quite like other kids, so perhaps it's no surprise that Sparrow Clubs is growing and successful. Sparrow Clubs is the nation's only youth-based charity using this powerful service-learning model of kids-helping-kids. Youth earn up to $10 per hour by doing community service to help their "sparrow" child, and they find a sense of purpose, empowerment, and belonging in the process.

How do Sparrow Clubs work? Kids in medical crisis (sparrows) are referred to Sparrow Clubs by the hospital or social workers, and become not only financial recipients, but also the focus of the service project. Youth work toward earning $2,560 in Sparrow Cash (initial seed money donated by sponsors) to help the sick child, earning up to $10 for every hour of community service completed. In addition, every dollar that youth raise or personally donate goes into their "sparrow's" designated fund. Adult volunteers facilitate the process, letting the youth lead. Sick kids get help. Healthy kids become heroes.

Can one kid make a difference in the world? Dameon did. As Sparrow Clubs expands its reach to help even more young people find their wings; we need your help. Sparrow Clubs needs funds to support growing service demands for the organization, to expand our programs, and to sponsor more "broken sparrows" like Michael in communities across our country.

HOW CAN YOU HELP?

Sparrow Clubs can continue to serve children, families, and communities; prevent the societal costs associated with disenfranchised youth (e.g. violence, pregnancy, and drug abuse); and foster safe havens for children and teens. But we need your help. We seek tax-deductible donations to:
Help sponsor Sparrow Clubs and kids,
Support our current programs, and
Expand our service capacity.

Young heroes need heroes like you.

Sparrow Clubs™
Changing lives. Saving lives.

Contact us at:

Sparrow Clubs
4192 NW 61st
Redmond, OR 97756
1-800-469-8542
www.sparrowclubs.org

Appendix Two

Appendix Two

40 Developmental Assets

Search Institute has identified the following building blocks of healthy development that help young people grow up healthy, caring, and responsible.

Category	Asset Name and Definition

External Assets

Support
1. Family Support-Family life provides high levels of love and support.
2. Positive Family Communication-Young person and her or his parent(s) communicate positively, and young person is willing to seek advice and counsel from parents.
3. Other Adult Relationships-Young person receives support from three or more nonparent adults.
4. Caring Neighborhood-Young person experiences caring neighbors.
5. Caring School Climate-School provides a caring, encouraging environment.
6. Parent Involvement in Schooling-Parent(s) are actively involved in helping young person succeed in school.

Empowerment
7. Community Values Youth-Young person perceives that adults in the community value youth.
8. Youth as Resources-Young people are given useful roles in the community.
9. Service to Others-Young person serves in the community one hour or more per week.
10. Safety-Young person feels safe at home, school, and in the neighborhood.

Boundaries & Expectations
11. Family Boundaries-Family has clear rules and consequences and monitors the young person's whereabouts.
12. School Boundaries-School provides clear rules and consequences.
13. Neighborhood Boundaries-Neighbors take responsibility for monitoring young people's behavior.
14. Adult Role Models-Parent(s) and other adults model positive, responsible behavior.
15. Positive Peer Influence-Young person's best friends model responsible behavior.
16. High Expectations-Both parent(s) and teachers encourage the young person to do well.

Constructive Use of Time
17. Creative Activities-Young person spends three or more hours per week in lessons or practice in music, theater, or other arts.
18. Youth Programs-Young person spends three or more hours per week in sports, clubs, or organizations at school and/or in the community.
19. Religious Community-Young person spends one or more hours per week in activities in a religious institution.
20. Time at Home-Young person is out with friends "with nothing special to do" two or fewer nights per week.

Internal Assets

Commitment to Learning
21. Achievement Motivation-Young person is motivated to do well in school.
22. School Engagement-Young person is actively engaged in learning.
23. Homework-Young person reports doing at least one hour of homework every school day.
24. Bonding to School-Young person cares about her or his school.
25. Reading for Pleasure-Young person reads for pleasure three or more hours per week.

Positive Values
26. Caring-Young person places high value on helping other people.
27. Equality and Social Justice-Young person places high value on promoting equality and reducing hunger and poverty.
28. Integrity-Young person acts on convictions and stands up for her or his beliefs.
29. Honesty-Young person "tells the truth even when it is not easy."
30. Responsibility-Young person accepts and takes personal responsibility.
31. Restraint-Young person believes it is important not to be sexually active or to use alcohol or other drugs.

Social Competencies
32. Planning and Decision Making-Young person knows how to plan ahead and make choices.
33. Interpersonal Competence-Young person has empathy, sensitivity, and friendship skills.
34. Cultural Competence-Young person has knowledge of and comfort with people of different cultural/racial/ethnic backgrounds.
35. Resistance Skills-Young person can resist negative peer pressure and dangerous situations.
36. Peaceful Conflict Resolution-Young person seeks to resolve conflict nonviolently.

Positive Identity
37. Personal Power-Young person feels he or she has control over "things that happen to me."
38. Self-Esteem-Young person reports having a high self-esteem.
39. Sense of Purpose-Young person reports that "my life has a purpose."
40. Positive View of Personal Future-Young person is optimistic about her or his personal future

Bibliography

Pages 16–17.
Excerpt from *Love Your God with All Your Mind* by J.P. Moreland, © 1997. Used by permission of NavPress—www.navpress.com. All rights reserved.

Pages 31–32.
Excerpt from *The Shattered Lantern* by Ronald Rolheiser © 2001 and The Crossroads Publishing Company. Reprinted by permission.

Page 63.
Excerpt from Benjamin Netanyahu speech reprinted by permission of Hillsdale College, IMPRIMUS.

Pages 85–86.
Excerpt from *New Seeds of Contemplation* by Thomas Merton, copyright © 1961 by The Abbey of Gethsemani, Inc. Reprinted by permission of New Directions Publishing Corp.

Page 106.
Excerpt from *C.S. Lewis for the Third Millenium* by Peter Kreeft, © 1994 Ignatius Press, San Francisco. Reprinted by permission.

Page 115.
STUFF THAT WORKS, Words and Music by Guy Clark and Rodney J. Crowell, © 1994 EMI APRIL MUSIC INC, GSC MUSIC and SONY/ATV TUNES LLC.All Rights for GSC MUSIC Controlled and Administered by EMI APRIL MUSIC INC. All Rights Reserved. International Copyright Secured. Used by Permission.

Page 121.
Excerpt of Emerging Answers: Research Findings on Programs to Reduce Teen Pregnancy, reprinted by permission of The National Campaign to Prevent Teen Pregnancy by Douglas Kirby, Ph.D. © May 2001.